Jesus Today

Daily Devotional
100 Days with Jesus Christ

2 Minutes A Day of Christian Bible Inspiration

Paul Backholer

Jesus Today
Daily Devotional
100 Days with Jesus Christ

Scripture quotations are taken from:
- NIV – The New International Version®. NIV®. Copyright © 1973, 1978, 1984 by International Bible Society. Used by permission of Zondervan. All rights reserved.
- NKJV – The New King James Version. Published by Thomas Nelson, Inc. Copyright © 1982 by Thomas Nelson, Inc. Used by permission. All rights reserved.
- AV – Authorised Version / King James Version.

ISBN 978-1-907066-35-1
British Library Cataloguing In Publication Data.
A Record of this Publication is available
from the British Library.

First published in 2014 by ByFaith Media.
Second edition © 2016.
Third edition © 2017.
This book is also available as an ebook.

- Jesus Christ is Lord -

Contents and Themes

Page

Introduction

I have often wondered what it must have been like to sit at Jesus' feet two thousand years ago, to listen to everything He said and taught. It must have been wonderful to see the Lord Jesus Christ and hear His voice, and yet we too are mightily blessed to have the records of our Lord's life and His promise – "Blessed are those who have not seen and yet have believed" (John 20:29). Luke set out, 'To write to you an orderly account' of Jesus' life (Luke 1:3), and John testified in his Gospel: 'These are written that you may believe that Jesus is the Christ, the Son of God and that believing you may have life in His name' (John 20:31).

As I was dwelling on the privilege of those who were present when Jesus taught, I felt compelled by the Holy Spirit to set aside my normal daily Bible routine, to study for a season, the words and teaching of Jesus alone. As I slowly went through the accounts of Jesus' life, ministry and teaching, the Holy Spirit glorified Christ (John 16:13-14), and it was an inspiring time, which birthed this book.

This daily devotional is compact and to the point. The idea is not to trawl through as much teaching as possible and quickly forget, but instead to, 'Let the Word of Christ dwell in you richly in all wisdom, teaching and admonishing' (Colossians 3:16).

This devotional begins by seeking who Jesus was and is; before we can follow His teaching, we need to be sure who is speaking (John 10:30); and it is not always chronological, as I have sought to put some themes together. Due to the fact that, 'All Scripture is given by inspiration of God' (2 Timothy 3:16), I have also included other relevant Scriptures to dovetail with the Lord's messages.

We may dream of sitting at Christ's feet, as the disciples did, but Jesus taught, "It is to your advantage that I go away; for if I do not go away, the Helper will not come to you; but if I depart, I will send Him to you" (John 16:7-8). The Lord Jesus explained that the Spirit of Christ (1 Peter 1:11), will open our hearts and minds to His teaching. "The Holy Spirit, whom the Father will send in My name, He will teach you all things and bring to your remembrance all things that I said to you" (John 14:26).

Day 1

When Time Began

'This is the disciple who testifies of these things and wrote these things; and we know that his testimony is true. And there are also many other things that Jesus did, which if they were written one by one, I suppose that even the world itself could not contain the books that would be written. Amen' (John 21:24-25).

Two thousand years ago a Man lived who changed the world. He was born into poverty and His family was forced to flee their nation, and became refugees. His parents were lower class, had no positions of influence in society and He received no formal education. He never traveled farther than two hundred miles from His home, never wrote a book, nor did He seek fame or power and He spent many years practically homeless. He gained no wealth, had no political opinions and the only man to hold a sword in His name, He rebuked – yet He was executed by the age of thirty-three.

In a world where most lives are quickly forgotten, this Man changed history – time began with Him. The remembrance of your birthday, of every life, and of all history, including the rise and fall of empires are defined by His life. His Words have inspired billions of people and His teaching has guided many of the world's most powerful people – defining nations, empires and civilisations.

The four chronicles of His life remain as the central masterpieces which bind the world's most successful book together; the Bible is the best seller this year and in every year. He is not only the Man who defines history, but according to John, He is the Founder and Creator of all. "In the beginning was the Word and the Word was with God, and the Word was God. He was in the beginning with God. All things were made through Him and without Him nothing was made that was made. In Him was life and the life was the light of men. And the light shines in the darkness, and the darkness did not comprehend it" (John 1:1-5).

His name is Jesus Christ; He wasn't just a man – He was and is God. Jesus said, "He who has seen Me has seen the Father" and, "I and My Father are One" (John 10:30, 14:9).

Day 2

A Progressive Revelation

"Where is He who has been born King of the Jews? For we have seen His star in the East and have come to worship Him" (Matthew 2:2).

The Bible is God's revelation to mankind (2 Timothy 3:16). In the Scriptures God has spoken and revealed who He is and what His plan for earth was and still is. In the sacred chronicles inspired by the Holy Spirit, God explains why we live in a world marred by sin, suffering and tragedy, and how He set about to redeem mankind and earth! The Bible is God's Word to us – 'For prophecy never came by the will of man, but holy men of God spoke as they were moved by the Holy Spirit' (2 Peter 1:20-21).

Thousands of years ago, God set aside one man, called him by name and changed his life, making him the father of a nation. His name was to be Abraham, the father of the Jews and from his revelation of God, and the insights the Lord gave to his descendants, we received the Bible.

Through Abraham and his descendants, God promised that the world would be blessed (Genesis 22:18), and from the seed of this man called by the Lord, came a people through whom God sent a Messiah to the world. 'Now the birth of Jesus Christ was as follows: After His mother Mary was betrothed to Joseph, before they came together, she was found with child of the Holy Spirit' (Matthew 1:18).

Jesus Christ came to earth as the bearer of great news – all who trusted in Him would receive forgiveness of sins and an inheritance with God in heaven. God appeared to Joseph saying, "You shall call His name Jesus, for He will save His people from their sins" (Matthew 1:21).

Isaiah the prophet foretold Christ's ministry on earth, as the One who would preach glad tidings to the poor and proclaim liberty to all who are captives to sin. The Lord's ministry, Isaiah foretold, would bring comfort to those who mourn and He would provide garments of praise to those who are burdened with the spirit of heaviness – giving them beauty for ashes. Christ did not come to destroy lives – He came to declare the acceptable year of the Lord (Isaiah 61:1-4).

Day 3

True Love is Sacrificial

"All should honour the Son just as they honour the Father. He who does not honour the Son does not honour the Father...the Father is in Me and I in Him" (John 5:23, 10:38).

After the birth of Jesus Christ, according to Jewish religious Law, Mary and Joseph were compelled to bring a sacrifice to the temple in Jerusalem, to present their firstborn Son to God. The Law required a lamb to be offered (Leviticus 12:6-8), but as a poor family they were permitted to bring the lesser sacrifices of, 'A pair of turtledoves or two young pigeons' (Luke 2:21-24).

Thus, on a sacred day, a poor family entered the temple with a Child, God Himself in disguise. Many were busy with religious duties, but two were close enough to the Holy Spirit to know God was present (Luke 2:25-38). Anna testified of Christ and Simeon prophesied by the Spirit, "My eyes have seen Your salvation which You have prepared before the face of all peoples, a light to bring revelation to the Gentiles and the glory of Your people Israel" (Luke 2:30-32).

Who was this Baby in the temple? God, 'Manifested in the flesh' (1 Timothy 3:16); 'For in Him dwells all the fullness of the Godhead bodily' (Colossians 2:9).

In the West we have become over familiar with the concept of Jesus Christ coming to earth. We have forgotten that the Creator came to love the created. The One who spoke life into being, came to suffer for that life. He loved us, not in words only, but by sacrificial actions (John 15:13).

When we think of God loving us, we must be careful to understand what God means by love. We may 'love' ice cream and so forth. We 'love' a person and then our feelings change. These descriptions of 'love' tell us nothing of God's love, or what Christian love should be. Jesus said, "As the Father loved Me, I also have loved you; abide in My love" (John 15:9-10). How has God loved us? The Son reduced Himself to be less than an angel to save man, made of dust. 'Jesus, who was made a little lower than the angels, for the suffering of death crowned with glory and honour, that He, by the grace of God, might taste death for all' (Hebrews 2:9).

Day 4

God is Real Love

"For God so loved the world that He gave His only begotten Son, that whoever believes in Him should not perish but have everlasting life. For God did not send His Son into the world to condemn the world, but that the world through Him might be saved" (John 3:16-17).

The word 'love' is greatly misunderstood in our culture and its meaning is depreciated by the English language. In the West, our most common theme of love is romantic love and at its heart romantic 'love' usually begins in selfishness. We love the lovely because we want to be loved in return. Our 'love' is grounded in 'how we feel' and if these feelings change, we may try to find someone 'more lovely' to love.

This concept of love is not biblical, nor can it truly be called love – a better description could be infatuation or romantic desire. Our understanding of love has been deflated by the carnal nature, because the love of God is *giving* in nature. 'God is love' (1 John 4:8), and when love is manifested – it does not seek its own, it is kind, it suffers long, is not proud or rude; it bears all things, endures all things and rejoices in the truth, etc. (1 Corinthians 13:4-8).

The world began in love. God loved and so He created the world, giving it to His Son (Colossians 1:16). Together, the Father and Son gave dominion of the world to man (Genesis 1:26-31, Luke 4:6). Yet, we afflicted God's gift (Genesis 3:1-24), and the, 'Creation was subjected to futility' (Romans 8:20). Nevertheless, out of His love, God planned to redeem mankind and began with a covenant with Abraham (Genesis 13:15). Then, God kept on giving, with the covenants made with Moses, David and Israel, to the legacy of His prophets. God suffered long in love and when mankind failed to obey, He sent Christ to do what man did not do (Hebrews 8:7-11).

God loves us not because we are lovely, but because He is love. We often try to avoid unlovely people and we think of 'falling in and out' of love; yet the most loving people are not those who are slaves to their feelings, but those who love like God, sacrificially. Why did Christ come to earth and suffer for us? Because He is love (1 John 4:19).

Day 5

The Subject Son

'So when they saw Him, they were amazed and His mother said to Him, "Son, why have You done this to us? Look, Your father and I have sought You anxiously." And He said to them, "Why did you seek Me? Did you not know that I must be about My Father's business?" ' (Luke 2:48-49).

When Jesus was twelve years of age, He went to the Feast of Passover with His family, and stayed behind to listen and ask questions about the Scriptures without His parents' knowledge (Luke 2:42-47). After three days they found Him and Jesus went home with them as a subject Son.

I sometimes wonder if Mary and Joseph questioned why their lives were so hard, considering all the revelations they had received. Two young people nursed and overcame a pregnancy scandal in their village, and at the worst time had to travel for a census. Then, when Mary's pregnancy came to fruition there was no room for them (Luke 2:7). They were forced to flee into Egypt and a massacre followed (Matthew 2:18). What was it like for them to travel and seek entrance into Roman Egypt? How harsh or kind was their daily lives?

After returning to Israel, Jesus experienced a normal home life. His father was a poor carpenter (Luke 2:22-24), and Jesus followed in the family business (Mark 6:3). Jesus was the firstborn son (Matthew 1:25), and brothers and sisters followed, including James, Joses, Judas and Simon (Mark 6:3). Imagine life in their busy home, with all those children and all the tedious work of life to be accomplished.

Sometime between the age of twelve and thirty, the young Jesus would have automatically become the head of this family when Joseph died (Luke 3:23). The responsibility to care for His mother Mary, was with Him all the way to the cross when He commissioned John saying, "Behold your mother," and from that hour he took her to his own home (John 19:27).

Jesus' miraculous ministry commenced after thirty invisible years, as He lived a very real and full human life, before His powerful ministry began. He was fully God and fully man.

Day 6

Baptised Into Death

'Jesus came from Galilee to John at the Jordan to be baptized by him. And John tried to prevent Him, saying, "I need to be baptized by You and are You coming to me?" But Jesus answered and said to him, "Permit it to be so now, for thus it is fitting for us to fulfil all righteousness." Then he allowed Him. When He had been baptized, Jesus came up immediately from the water and behold, the heavens were opened to Him, and He saw the Spirit of God descending like a dove and alighting upon Him. Suddenly a voice came from heaven, saying, "This is My beloved Son, in whom I am well pleased" ' (Matthew 3:13-17).

Jesus Christ's ministry commenced in humility. The One who knew no sin, who had nothing to repent for or confess, embraced a baptism of repentance and set a precedent for all who would follow Him. Paul clarified the Lord's ministry, compared to the first sinful man: 'The first man was of the earth (Adam), made of dust; the second Man (Christ), is the Lord from heaven' (1 Corinthians 15:47). 'For He made Him who knew no sin, to be sin for us, that we might become the righteousness of God in Him' (2 Corinthians 5:21).

God's response to Christ's humility was to speak audibly and confirm to all, the Sonship and obedience of Christ, "This is My beloved Son, in whom I am well pleased."

The Bible exhorts all to follow Christ's example of humility. 'Let this mind be in you which was also in Christ Jesus, who, being in the form of God, did not consider it robbery to be equal with God, but made Himself of no reputation, taking the form of a bondservant and coming in the likeness of men. And being found in appearance as a man, He humbled Himself and became obedient to the point of death, even the death of the cross. Therefore God also has highly exalted Him and given Him the name which is above every name, that at the name of Jesus every knee should bow, of those in heaven, and of those on earth and of those under the earth, and that every tongue should confess that Jesus Christ is Lord, to the glory of God the Father' (Philippians 2:5-11).

Day 7

The Battle Begins

'Then Jesus was led up by the Spirit into the wilderness to be tempted by the devil' (Matthew 4:1).

Many people are inclined to believe that they can discern all reality by utilising their five senses. They think what they see, touch, hear, smell and taste gives them the ability to find out what is real. However, Jesus presents all with their need for a spiritual awakening (John 3:6). Paul wrote: 'But the natural man does not receive the things of the Spirit of God, for they are foolishness to him; nor can he know them, because they are spiritually discerned' (1 Corinthians 2:14).

Christ the Lord was led by the Holy Spirit into a spiritual battle, waged on earth, which could only be 'seen' or discerned in the Spirit. 'For we do not wrestle against flesh and blood, but against principalities, against powers, against the rulers of the darkness of this age, against spiritual hosts of wickedness in the heavenly places' (Ephesians 6:12).

The devil is not a cartoon character with a pitchfork, but a fallen angel. Jesus said, "I saw Satan fall like lightning from heaven" (Luke 10:18). Here Christ opens our eyes to eternal reality; He tells us there is another world, which we cannot discern with our human senses. In that spiritual world, God is present with His angels, (and demons live in an unseen realm too). It is to a part of this spiritual world, which we call heaven, where our eternal lives will be fully manifested.

The Bible explains Satan was once an archangel, created by God to serve Him (Isaiah 14:12-15). This angel rebelled and became a distorted being, the original source of all temptation, evil and suffering (Job 1:12-22, 2:4-8, James 1:13). By tricking the first humans, Satan was able to steal their delegated authority or dominion over earth (Genesis 1:26, Luke 4:6), leading to devastation. This is why Jesus called Satan, "The ruler of this world" (John 12:31), and Jesus came to, 'Destroy the works of the devil' (1 John 3:8).

In the wilderness, Jesus commenced a great battle with Satan and the Lord also portrays his final defeat. Jesus said, "Depart from Me, you cursed, into the everlasting fire prepared for the devil and his angels" (Matthew 25:41-42).

Day 8

The Temptation of Christ

'Now when the tempter came to Him, he said, "If You are the Son of God, command that these stones become bread." But Jesus answered and said, "It is written, 'Man shall not live by bread alone, but by every Word that proceeds from the mouth of God" ' (Matthew 4:3-4).

Jesus experienced three temptations by Satan and each enticement reveals a great deal about the way Satan fights against us. The first temptation was against the weakened flesh of Christ, the second was to test God and the third was to compromise on fulfilling God's ultimate will.

When Christ's human body was weak through fasting, Satan tempted Him to prove His authority and status, to use His power as God, to turn stones into bread. Satan urged Jesus to use His Divine power, rather than feeding directly from God. 'But He answered and said, "It is written, 'Man shall not live by bread alone, but by every Word that proceeds from the mouth of God" ' (Matthew 4:4).

In Satan's second temptation, he urged Christ to put God the Father to the test, to do a supernatural work to protect Him. Satan often tempts us to test God and ask for signs – "Do something to prove..." But this is not faith in action (Hebrews 11:1). Jesus said to Thomas, "Blessed are those who have not seen and yet have believed" (John 20:29). To overcome Satan, Jesus said, "It is written again, 'You shall not tempt the Lord your God' " (Matthew 4:7).

In each temptation Jesus quoted the written Word of God to defeat Satan (Hebrews 2:18). If we wish to overcome with Jesus, we too must know the Bible and how to quote it. Peter reminds us that Satan is like a lion, stalking his prey and ready to pounce. He warns believers to resist Satan, to acknowledge his attacks as real, to look out for them and to engage in spiritual warfare. 'Be sober, be vigilant; because your adversary the devil walks about like a roaring lion, seeking whom he may devour. Resist him, steadfast in the faith, knowing that the same sufferings are experienced by your brotherhood in the world' (1 Peter 5:8-9).

Day 9

The Third Temptation

'The devil took Jesus up on an exceedingly high mountain, and showed Him all the kingdoms of the world and their glory. And he said to Him, "All these things I will give You if You will fall down and worship me." Then Jesus said to him, "Away with you, Satan! For it is written, 'You shall worship the Lord your God and Him only you shall serve.' " Then the devil left Him' (Matthew 4:8-10).

In Christ, God had come to Israel and invaded the domain of Satan, to deliver all who put their trust in God. Satan, 'The god of this age' (2 Corinthians 4:4), therefore tempted the Lord in the wilderness, when He was subject to all human weaknesses (Matthew 4:2). Thus, before the visible ministry of Jesus began, Satan gave Jesus an offer which he hoped the Lord would not refuse. Christ knew Satan held the legal right to be the 'ruler of this world' (John 12:31), because the fall had given him this power. But now Christ came to earth, 'That through death, He might destroy him who had the power of death, that is, the devil' (Hebrews 2:14). Yet Satan appeared to offer Christ His objectives without the cross.

Notice in this temptation, Jesus did not challenge Satan's right to give Him all the kingdoms of the world, because by submitting to Satan's temptation, the first humans gave their authority on earth to the evil one (Genesis 1:28, Luke 4:6). But Christ resisted this and every temptation of Satan, the serpent who, 'Deceives the nations' (Revelation 12:9, 20:3), by submitting to the Word of God. Satan is undermined by the authority of Scripture and Christ's mission to destroy the works of the enemy was completed by faith alone.

Jesus later announced, "Now is the judgment of this world; now the ruler of this world will be cast out" (John 12:31). Jesus refused to heed Satan's temptations and He took back the keys of death and hell by obeying His Father (Revelation 1:18). When Jesus' mission on earth was later completed, Christ said Paul's call was to turn people, "From darkness to light and from the power of Satan to God, that they may receive forgiveness of sins and an inheritance among those who are sanctified by faith in Me" (Acts 26:18).

Day 10

Repentance and the Kingdom of God

'Jesus began to preach and to say, "Repent, for the Kingdom of Heaven is at hand" ' (Matthew 4:17).

After overcoming all of Satan's misleading temptations, the first message Jesus preached was twofold in nature; repent and the Kingdom of Heaven is at hand.

Christ's Kingdom is the eternal Kingdom (Daniel 2:44-45), which grows on earth as people put their faith in Jesus, and this Kingdom continues in heaven and will one day be manifested in full on earth. The book of Revelation foretells a time when, "The kingdoms of this world have become the kingdoms of our Lord and of His Christ, and He shall reign forever and ever!" (Revelation 11:15).

To be part of this Kingdom we must repent, which means to turn away from sin – to do an about turn. Instead of self being the centre of our lives, Christ and His will should be enthroned in our hearts (John 14:15).

When we invest our faith to believe in the power of Jesus Christ's resurrection, we are, 'Delivered from the power of darkness and conveyed into the Kingdom of the Son of His love, in whom we have redemption through His blood, the forgiveness of sins' (Colossians 1:13-14). Through faith, we receive citizenship of Christ's Kingdom and are part of His living Kingdom on earth, awaiting heaven (Ephesians 2:19).

To be a faithful citizen, we must behave like one. We are no longer a part of this world, but pilgrims, seeking a better home (Ephesians 2:12, Hebrews 11:13). The gospel of the Kingdom now means the gospel of Christ's governance in our hearts and lives. This was the message Christ preached (Matthew 4:23, 9:35, 24:14, Mark 1:15). He came to be our King and He will return to be King of all (Luke 1:33, Romans 15:12, 1 Corinthians 15:25, Revelation 11:15). 'For unto us a Child is born, unto us a Son is given...of His government and peace there shall be no end' (Isaiah 9:6-7).

Christ came to destroy the works of the devil and sin is Satan's domain. Citizens of the Kingdom of God must reject sin (1 John 3:8), because righteousness is truth and the devil resists all truth (John 8:44, 1 John 5:17).

Day 11

The Domain of Christ

'Then Jesus returned in the power of the Spirit to Galilee, and news of Him went out through all the surrounding region...and He healed them' (Luke 4:14-15, 40).

Jesus' ministry commenced with a baptism of humility, followed by being led by the Holy Spirit into the wilderness to be tested, where Christ overcame Satan. Then, the Light of the World emerged to challenge and overcome the Kingdom of Darkness. Isaiah foresaw these events and described them by the Holy Spirit, "The people who sat in darkness have seen a great light, and upon those who sat in the region and shadow of death light has dawned." From that time Jesus began to preach and to say, "Repent, for the Kingdom of Heaven is at hand" (Matthew 4:16-17).

The Kingdom of Heaven or the Kingdom of God means Christ's dominion over all and in all. The Lord Jesus invites us to receive His Lordship in every area of our lives, so we may truly be, 'In the Kingdom of God.' The extension of Christ's Kingdom on earth continues when we freely submit to Jesus and invite others to do the same.

Jesus sought out disciples and announced, "Follow Me, and I will make you fishers of men" (Matthew 4:19). What were the disciples to do? They were to follow Christ, learn from Him and obey, as He challenged the power of Satan on earth. This power was manifested by Christ to set people free from sin and save them from Satan's Kingdom.

'Jesus went about all Galilee, teaching in their synagogues, preaching the gospel of the Kingdom, and healing all kinds of sickness and all kinds of disease among the people. Then His fame went throughout all Syria; and they brought to Him all sick people who were afflicted with various diseases and torments, and those who were demon-possessed and paralytics; and He healed them' (Matthew 4:23-25).

God rules in the hearts of those who choose to freely follow Him. All in His Kingdom can be delivered from the power of evil and forgiven (Colossians 1:13). One day, He shall return again to re-take earth in glory (Mark 13:26). 'But now we do not yet see all things put under Him' (Hebrews 2:8).

Day 12

The Good News of the Kingdom of God

"The Spirit of the Lord God is upon Me, because He has anointed Me to preach the gospel to the poor. He has sent Me to heal the broken hearted, to proclaim liberty to the captives and recovery of sight to the blind, to set at liberty those who are oppressed; to proclaim the acceptable year of the Lord" (Luke 4:18-19).

If a missionary spoke to someone who had never heard of Jesus, he or she could speak with biblical authority saying something like this, "I have come to bring you good news. God, the Almighty Creator of all, has seen you, and heard your silent cries and prayers (Acts 7:34). He has seen your sadness, suffering and all which has hurt you, and He loves you with an everlasting love (Jeremiah 31:3).

"God sent His Son Jesus from heaven to earth, to become a man, to heal the broken hearted, to proclaim liberty to the captives of sin and deliverance from all evil. Jesus came to comfort all who mourn, to give them beauty for the ashes of their lives and joy to replace mourning (Isaiah 61:1-3).

"Jesus came to earth to pay the debt for your sin, so you can be His child and joint heir in His eternal Kingdom in heaven (Galatians 4:7). Through faith in Jesus' death and resurrection, God's only Son, you can now be forgiven for every sin you have ever committed, and made righteous by faith (Philippians 3:9). Even now, God wants to build a relationship with you and a mansion for you in heaven; if you will repent and receive Christ as your Saviour and Lord."

Jesus said, "In My Father's house are many mansions; if it were not so, I would have told you. I go to prepare a place for you" (John 14:2-3). When Jesus spoke of mansions, His listeners probably had in mind the large Roman villas, where many mansions or spacious apartments were linked together in one house, with a courtyard in the middle. Christ's teaching reminds us that heaven is real and we can all have an eternal home with Him, if we accept His free invitation. 'Thanks be to God for His indescribable gift!' (2 Corinthians 9:15). Are you a member of Jesus' family?

Day 13

Have You Been Born Again?

'Jesus said to him, "Most assuredly, I say to you, unless one is born again, he cannot see the Kingdom of God." Nicodemus said to Him, "How can a man be born when he is old? Can he enter a second time into his mother's womb and be born?" Jesus answered, "Most assuredly, I say to you, unless one is born of water and the Spirit, he cannot enter the Kingdom of God. That which is born of the flesh is flesh and that which is born of the Spirit is spirit. Do not marvel that I said to you, 'You must be born again' " (John 3:3-7).

When the first humans sinned against God they gave their authority on the earth to Satan and things changed within them too (Genesis 1:26-28, Luke 4:6, Romans 5:14, 1 Corinthians 15:22). They died spiritually. God had said, "You shall not...lest you die" (Genesis 3:3). Therefore, when they sinned, their relationships with God ceased and additionally, their bodies became subject to the process of corruption, decay, disease and death (1 Corinthians 15:21-22, 42-45).

When Christ spoke to Nicodemus He explained the remedy for the fall of man (Romans 3:23). We are all born once in the flesh and we also need to be born again in our spirit. The spiritual part of our beings must be re-awakened and born again. Jesus drew a distinction between the body and the spirit within the body. He said, "That which is born of the flesh is flesh and that which is born of the Spirit is spirit."

How can your spirit be awakened and born again? Jesus said, "You believe in God, believe also in Me" (John 14:1-2). Paul explained: 'If you confess with your mouth the Lord Jesus and believe in your heart that God has raised Him from the dead, you will be saved. For with the heart one believes unto righteousness and with the mouth confession is made unto salvation' (Romans 10:9-10).

When we enter into purging repentance and follow Christ's pathway of deliverance to freedom in Him, the Holy Spirit will respond and seal us for the day of salvation, as our spirits are born again (Ephesians 4:30). Have you repented, believed and confessed faith in Christ?

Day 14

The Greatest Love Story

"As the Father loved Me, I also have loved you; abide in My love. If you keep My commandments, you will abide in My love, just as I have kept My Father's commandments and abide in His love" (John 15:9-10).

Christianity is the greatest love story of all eternity. From before time began, God saw you and loved you (Ephesians 1:4). On the first day of your life, with your first breath, His plans for your life were brooding over you (Ephesians 2:10). He loved you when you did not know His name, and when you first sensed His voice and will, and rejected it, He loved you still. When you searched for satisfaction in every other possible place, He continued to love you and called to you (John 16:8). God says, "Yes, I have loved you with an everlasting love; therefore with loving kindness I have drawn you" (Jeremiah 31:3). Jesus said, "For God did not send His Son into the world to condemn the world, but that the world through Him might be saved" (John 3:17).

As a result of His love, when you finally purged your heart in repentance before God and put your faith in Jesus Christ the Lord, He did not scold you, but welcomed you with perfect love. As prodigal's, we all receive a grace filled reception from a loving Father to His prodigal son. "He arose and came to his father. But when he was still a great way off, his father saw him and had compassion, and ran and fell on his neck and kissed him" (Luke 15:20).

God's love is great; even if you turned your back on Him to flirt and commit adultery with the world; He was still prepared to take you back to Himself when you came in sincere repentance. Even if He was the last choice you considered, He was still willing to accept you, as if He was your first. As long as you come to Him with a repentant and penitent heart, His mercy has no end. 'If we confess our sins, He is faithful and just to forgive us our sins, and to cleanse us from all unrighteousness' (1 John 1:9-10).

His love is free, whilst our love for Him is proved by our actions. "If you love Me, keep My commandments," says the Lord (John 14:15), and we will then abide in His love.

Day 15

God's Plan A, For Life

"It is the Spirit who gives life; the flesh profits nothing. The words that I speak to you are spirit and they are life" (John 6:63).

The Bible and the teaching of the Lord Jesus Christ is our guide, to what could be called, Plan A Living. Through His parables, lessons and spiritual guidance, the Lord has told us what works and what can never work in life. He never tries to take the best from us; but He does tell us to flee from all that will harm (John 8:35). Many of us have spent much time seeking after things which turned out to be empty and now Christ offers us abundant living in Him.

In some ways, believers in Jesus Christ are called to learn how to rediscover the lost paradise of Eden within. On earth, we still live on the outside of God's eternal paradise, but deep within our spirit, by the power of the abiding presence of the Holy Spirit, the living water of Christ can bring re-birth and flourishing growth (John 7:37-39).

Learning how to enter into Plan A Living will take time, as we submit our spirit to God, and allow the Holy Spirit to re-train us to think and live in Christ. The Lord wants the best for us all; even now God may be saying to you, "You've done it your way for so long; are you now ready to surrender and learn how I want you to live? My way is the road to abundant living, where all you need is found in Christ by the power of the abiding presence of the Holy Spirit."

Plan A Living is Jesus living; it occurs when we remove ourselves from the inner throne of self, and invite Jesus to come and take the throne of our hearts. In John 10, the Lord explains where Plan A leads, and who is the author of Plan B, C, D, etc, and what the other outcomes are. Jesus said, "I am the door of the sheep. All who ever came before Me are thieves and robbers…I am the door. If anyone enters by Me, he will be saved, and will go in and out and find pasture. The thief does not come except to steal and to kill and to destroy. I have come that they may have life and that they may have it more abundantly. I am the Good Shepherd. The Good Shepherd gives His life for the sheep" (John 10:7-12).

Day 16

The Way, Truth and Life

Jesus said, "I am the Way, the Truth and the Life. No one comes to the Father except through Me. If you had known Me, you would have known My Father also; and from now on you know Him and have seen Him" (John 14:6-7).

Christianity is either all true or all false. There is no other position which is acceptable (John 1:17). When the Truth, Christ Himself speaks to us His eternal truth, we must wake up and listen to His alarm. Jesus said, "Listen!" (Mark 4:3), "Take Heed," (Matthew 18:10) and, "Let these words sink down into your ears" (Luke 9:44). Do we listen to Jesus?

The devil, through the world is trying to send believers into an eternal sleep, as the prince of the power of the air bombards our culture with falsehoods (Ephesians 2:2), trying to drive us away from all truth and Christ's teaching.

However, with the loud beeping sound of the alarm clock of Christ's words, we can be raised out of our demonic, worldly sleep and face the daylight of His Word (1 John 2:15). It may hurt our hearts at first, but reality must be faced, for it is reality! Christ's words are true; all the world is a lie. John explained: 'We know that we are of God and the whole world lies under the sway of the wicked one' (1 John 5:19).

Jesus is the Way to God the Father, He is the embodiment of Truth, and in Him and through faith in Him, we can obtain eternal Life. Jesus said, "I give them eternal life and they shall never perish; neither shall anyone snatch them out of My hand" (John 10:28). Thus, it is impossible to find God the Father, except by going through Jesus and placing our faith in Him (Hebrews 10:19-23). All other routes, as the apostles taught, lead to another spirit (1 John 2:22, 4:3, 2 John 7).

Some have claimed the disciples never believed Jesus was God; this is not true. In the Gospels they wrote records of Jesus being worshipped more than ten times. In a boat they worshipped Him as God (Matthew 14:33), after He rose from the dead they worshipped Him (Matthew 28:9, 17), and when He ascended into heaven they worshipped Him (Luke 24:52). Peter refused worship (Acts 10:25-26), but not Jesus, who was worshipped by many (Mark 5:6, John 9:38).

Day 17

You Can Hear God's Voice

"My sheep hear My voice and I know them, and they follow Me. And I give them eternal life and they shall never perish; neither shall anyone snatch them out of My hand" (John 10:27-29).

In Old Testament times only the prophets, priests or great men and women of faith heard from God. In those days the voice of God was mostly distant or fearful (Hebrews 12:18). But today Jesus gives every believer the chance of having a close and intimate relationship with God (James 4:8).

The Lord specifically promises believers can, "Hear My voice." No born again believer in Jesus Christ, who has received the infilling of the Holy Spirit (Acts 2:1-4, 38-39), should need to say, "I have never heard from God." If you are a believer in Jesus, you confessed faith because you heard from God! Jesus said, "No one can come to Me unless the Father who sent Me draws him" (John 6:44). The reason you became a Christian is due to the fact that God's Spirit spoke deep down in your heart and drew you to Him.

The first contact you had with God was the inward conviction of the Holy Spirit, who was drawing you to seek God the Father (John 16:8-11), and then you found Christ, the Door. After you put your faith in Jesus (Romans 10:9), you received the seal of the Holy Spirit in your heart. 'In Him you also trusted, after you heard the word of truth, the gospel of your salvation; in whom also, having believed, you were sealed with the Holy Spirit of promise, who is the guarantee of our inheritance' (Ephesians 1:13-14).

Many expect God to speak to them in a way similar to Moses at the burning bush; yet God's witness is mostly in the inner man (1 Kings 19:12). He is communicating with us when we sense He is grieved by sin. 'Do not grieve the Holy Spirit of God, by whom you were sealed for the day of redemption' (Ephesians 4:30). Do we heed His inner voice?

Before we can hear God say, "Go," we must first hear Him say, "No," as He leads us away from sin, into holiness (Ephesians 5:1-7). If we refuse to hear Him, He will become distant and we may say, "God never speaks to me."

Day 18

Making Time To Hear God's Inner Voice

"But you, when you pray, go into your room and when you have shut your door, pray to your Father who is in the secret place; and your Father who sees in secret will reward you openly" (Matthew 6:6-7).

Once I was on a remote island in Papua New Guinea, in the Pacific and one of the chiefs asked me to greet the Queen of Britain. It took me some time to explain to the man that the Queen is the Monarch of more than sixty million citizens in Britain and many more in the commonwealth, and is unable to meet with everyone, including me. He was very surprised and said, "But she is your chief!" As I thought about this later, I realised the wonder that God in heaven, the Great Chief and King of all, has all the time in the world for us. If we are willing, we can meet with Him at any time!

If we are going to learn to be sensitive to the Holy Spirit, we must follow the teaching of Jesus and set aside time to pray, and silence the voices of the world. We live in an age of noise, which fears silence, because it is often in the silence God speaks, convicts us of sin, and deep inside He shows us our desperation. Several times in the Gospels we have a record of Jesus going to a deserted place to spend time with His Father. He needed quiet time with God and we also need to find a place of rest to hear from Him. 'There remains therefore a rest for the people of God. For he who has entered His rest has himself also ceased from his works as God did from His' (Hebrews 4:9-10).

It is impossible for any relationship to flourish if the people involved refuse to spend time together and it is the same with our relationship with God. James wrote: 'Draw near to God and He will draw near to you' (James 4:8). Here we have a promise and a lesson. If we choose to set aside the time to draw near to God and seek His face, just as Jesus did, He shall be found by us. Nevertheless, the Holy Spirit is waiting for us to make the first step to draw closer to God. It was the Spirit of God who first convicted us of sin and drew us to Jesus Christ, now He waits for us to prove our sincerity by drawing near to God (Zechariah 1:3).

Day 19

You are Loved

"Are not five sparrows sold for two copper coins? And not one of them is forgotten before God. But the very hairs of your head are all numbered. Do not fear therefore; you are of more value than many sparrows" (Luke 12:6-7).

On this planet there are no worthless, second-hand, third rate people. Every person has been created in the image of God and even though this image has been marred by the fall of mankind (Jeremiah 17:9, Mark 7:21), it is God's will not only to restore what was lost in Eden, but to give us more (1 John 3:1). 'For as in Adam all die, even so in Christ all shall be made alive' (1 Corinthians 15:22-23).

To the dictators of the world people are cheap and expendable. In contrast, we find that God cares for all, to the extent that He keeps a record of the number of hairs on each head. This preciseness and intimate knowledge God has of us, should bring great cheer to our hearts.

In Western culture, we have been taught that our value is found in what we do. Christianity teaches contrary to this, as our worth is not found in our temporal status, but who we are in Christ. If you are a Christian, then you are a child of God, chosen from before the foundation of the world. You are a son or daughter, an heir of Christ (Romans 8:17, Galatians 4:7). You were created in the image of God and His handiwork is found in all you are. Your life and every life is precious; this is why Christians cannot accept abortion. God was at work in our mothers' wombs, before our births.

'For You formed my inward parts; You covered me in my mother's womb. I will praise You, for I am fearfully and wonderfully made; marvellous are Your works and that my soul knows very well. My frame was not hidden from You, when I was made in secret and skilfully wrought in the lowest parts of the earth. Your eyes saw my substance, being yet unformed. And in Your book they all were written, the days fashioned for me, when as yet there were none of them. How precious also are Your thoughts to me, O God! How great is the sum of them! If I should count them, they would be more in number than the sand' (Psalm 139:13-18).

Day 20

Our First Love

'Then one of the scribes came and having heard them reasoning together, perceiving that He had answered them well, asked Him, "Which is the first commandment of all?" Jesus answered him, "The first of all the commandments is: 'Hear, O Israel, the Lord our God, the Lord is One. And you shall love the Lord your God with all your heart, with all your soul, with all your mind, and with all your strength.' This is the first commandment" ' (Mark 12:28-30).

How can we demonstrate our love for God? In Jesus' teaching we learn we must love God with the entirety of our hearts, with every fibre of our souls, with every area of our minds and with every part of our strength. He is to be our first and foremost love, and our love for Christ Jesus will be demonstrated by our obedience to all He commands. Jesus said, "He who does not love Me does not keep My Words; and the Word which you hear is not Mine but the Father's who sent Me" (John 14:24).

God is to be our first love, our last love and our only eternal love (Romans 12:1-2). There is only so much human beings can offer to others before they find the limited resources from which they draw, but not God. God's love is unlimited. John wrote: 'Behold what manner of love the Father has bestowed on us, that we should be called children of God' (1 John 3:1). As believers, we are not unwilling slaves of God, but His children and we should love as such.

How can we love God? Jesus said, "As the Father loved Me, I also have loved you; abide in My love. If you keep My commandments, you will abide in My love, just as I have kept My Father's commandments and abide in His love" (John 15:9-10). Obedience to Jesus expresses our love.

When we love God with all our heart, soul, mind and strength, He becomes the absolute centre of all we are. His will and desires become ours. His worldview will define ours and our supreme aim will be to demonstrate our love for Him in the way He showed us – by obeying Him as we, "Observe all things" Christ has commanded us (Matthew 28:20).

Day 21

We Love Because He is Love

"Greater love has no one than this, than to lay down one's life for his friends" (John 15:13).

God's desire is to find people who will freely love Him with everything they are and have. Jesus said, "The first of all the commandments is…, 'You shall love the Lord your God with all your heart, with all your soul, with all your mind and with all your strength' " (Mark 12:29-30).

In creation, God could have made a world filled with robots pre-programmed to obey and love Him, but if God had done that, those robots would have never truly loved Him. Would you feel loved by a computer which was programmed to say nice things to you, even though it has no heart or choice?

God gave mankind the greatest gift of all, free will. Being free and naturally independent – able to think, choose and believe what we like – means we are also able to rebel against God's will and reject Him.

God's will for Adam and Eve was for them to love and obey freely; instead they rebelled and sinned. Thus, mankind was stricken from God and cast out of paradise (Genesis 3:22-24). By choosing to align themselves against the will of God they cut themselves off from His life source and all joy. At this stage, God could have destroyed earth and started again, but if God was to find people who would love Him freely, they would also need their liberty of heart. Therefore, God's answer to this enigma was manifest in the sacrifice of Christ. Christ came to earth in love, to lay down His life, which produced a response from us which God desired.

John explains how Christ's sacrifice solved the conundrum of how to get free people to love God with all their heart. People at liberty cannot be forced to love, but sacrificial love can lead to a response. 'We love Him because He first loved us' (1 John 4:19). 'Behold what manner of love the Father has bestowed on us, that we should be called children of God!' (1 John 3:1). 'By this we know love, because He laid down His life for us' (1 John 3:16). Thus, God created a world in which free people would voluntarily love Him, in response to His, "Greater love" in Christ.

Day 22

The Kingdom Prepared Before Time Began

"Then the King will say to those on His right hand, 'Come, you blessed of My Father, inherit the Kingdom prepared for you from the foundation of the world' " (Matthew 25:34).

Why did God allow the earth He created as good, to be spoiled by us? We learn from the Bible that only free people can truly be at liberty to love God, and knowing that many would respond freely to Christ's love, God allowed mankind to sin and spoil His creation (Romans 8:19-23). But God still said, "What is this you have done?" (Genesis 3:13). God always knew man would fall in sin (Revelation 13:8), and in preparation, He designed a plan of redemption, "From the foundation of the world," to give us Kingdom citizenship.

The fall of man was a disaster for mankind, but in the long run God planned to turn a manmade tragedy into Christ's miracle. He chose us, who would freely choose Him, 'Before the foundation of the world' (Ephesians 1:4), and, 'Where sin abounded, grace abounded much more' (Romans 5:20).

Through the death and resurrection of Jesus, God is not only going to restore what was lost in Eden; He is doing far more! Redeemed believers will be more glorious than fallen Adam. We fell as created beings; we will rise in the likeness of the resurrection (Romans 6:5). We were made out of the dust, but our end is to be in Christ's image (1 John 3:2). We were created lower than the angels; in the future we will judge angels (1 Corinthians 6:3, Hebrews 2:6-8). In Adam we were dust made man, in Christ we are God's children and heirs (Hebrews 2:13, Romans 8:17).

God in His foreknowledge and sovereign will allowed the fall of man, in order for heaven to be inhabited by people who will love God by their free will choice, and these people will also share in superior honours than Adam.

At least eleven times in the Bible God reveals His plans are from, 'Before the foundation of the world.' He chose us (Ephesians 1:4), and fulfilled His plan before man even walked on earth (Hebrews 4:3, 1 Peter 1:20, Revelation 13:8). Before we sinned, God saw the fall and prepared His remedy, redemption and reviving us to more glorious things!

Day 23

Heaven Is Real

"Rejoice and be exceedingly glad, for great is your reward in heaven" (Matthew 5:12).

There are places all over the world which we have never been to, nor will we ever visit; and yet we know they are real because we have eyewitness accounts of them. We accept the reality of the testimonies we receive, because they are eyewitnesses of real locations we have never seen. Christ is our eyewitness of the reality of heaven; He is the One who came from heaven and returned to it (John 1:51, 6:38). Jesus said, "No one has ascended to heaven but He who came down from heaven, that is, the Son of Man" (John 3:13). The Holy Spirit also testifies of the reality of heaven and has given revelations to many prophets, apostles and believers of God's eternal home (1 Corinthians 2:9-12). It is in heaven that Jesus is preparing mansions for all who believe and trust in Him (John 14:1-4).

On the Mount of Transfiguration, Moses and Elijah stepped out of heaven to earth to speak with Christ (Matthew 17:1-4). One day, believers in Jesus shall take the same leap in the opposite direction, from this mortal world we will step into the eternal realm of God; and it is in that world, where Christ lives, where we will be rewarded by God.

Let us be very clear. Heaven is as real as any other place we have ever visited, or hope to visit. One of the reasons I wrote the book *Heaven – A Journey to Paradise*, was to explain how vivid and real the eternal land is.

Heaven is not pie in the sky, it is home. When we became believers in Jesus, we immediately received citizenship of heaven. 'Now, therefore, you are no longer strangers and foreigners (of heaven), but fellow citizens with the saints and members of the household of God' (Ephesians 2:19).

Jesus said, "Therefore whoever confesses Me before men, him I will also confess before My Father who is in heaven," and, "It has been given to you to know the mysteries of the Kingdom of Heaven" (Matthew 10:32, 13:11).

Day 24

Hell Is Real

"I say to you, My friends, do not be afraid of those who kill the body and after that have no more that they can do. But I will show you whom you should fear: Fear Him who, after He has killed, has power to cast into hell; yes, I say to you, fear Him!" (Luke 12:4-5).

Jesus spoke of the dangers of hell on a regular basis and urged all to flee to Him for salvation. He taught that hell is, "The everlasting fire prepared for the devil and his angels" (Matthew 25:41). It was never God's will for any person to go to hell because it was designed for the punishment of the devil and his demons. However, people will go there who choose to reject God's grace in stubborn self-will.

Christ explains in one parable how people will refuse His offer of eternal salvation. "But his citizens hated him and sent a delegation after him, saying, 'We will not have this man to reign over us' " (Luke 19:14). Hell is what many people believe they want – a life of total independence from God and the complete absence of God. What they forget is that everything we love on earth is merely a reflection of God. What will be left in hell, is all that is not God, 'The blackness of darkness forever' (2 Peter 2:17, Jude 13).

Christ tells us it is better for us to lose all, rather than go to hell. In a famous passage, He does not encourage us to hurt our physical bodies, but to crucify the sinful desires of the flesh and to die to them (Romans 13:14). Jesus said, "If your hand causes you to sin, cut it off. It is better for you to enter into life maimed, rather than having two hands, to go to hell, into the fire that shall never be quenched, where, 'Their worm does not die and the fire is not quenched.' And if your foot causes you to sin, cut it off. It is better for you to enter life lame, rather than having two feet, to be cast into hell, into the fire that shall never be quenched, where, 'Their worm does not die and the fire is not quenched.' And if your eye causes you to sin, pluck it out. It is better for you to enter the Kingdom of God with one eye, rather than having two eyes, to be cast into hell fire, where, 'Their worm does not die and the fire is not quenched' " (Mark 9:43-48).

Day 25

The Upside-Down Kingdom

'Seeing the multitudes, He went up on a mountain and when He was seated His disciples came to Him. Then He opened His mouth and taught them, saying: "Blessed are the poor in spirit, for theirs is the Kingdom of Heaven. Blessed are those who mourn..." ' (Matthew 5:1-3).

The Lord's Kingdom is in complete contrast with the accepted ways and standards of this world. Christ's Sermon on the Mount is the greatest message of defiance to human nature. In His sermon, He identifies the difference between the Christ nature and self-centred human nature. Jesus thus confirms the existence of another eternal Kingdom, where all the rules of earth are turned upside down.

In the world, it is often those who are arrogant, selfish and full of pride who reach the top (Job 21:7), and they often treat with contempt people below them, hurting and profiting from them. But in the heavenly upside-down Kingdom of God, those who are despised, selfless and loving will be eternally blessed. God sees all we do and will ultimately reward us for living according to His will – which is often the complete opposite of what the world expects. To be rewarded in God's eternal Kingdom, we must climb down towards the lowliest, to become childlike in our faith and humble in spirit. It is the overlooked who God sees.

God's Kingdom, its values, standards, morals and beliefs are often in total contrast to the world's because, 'The whole world lies under the sway of the wicked one' (1 John 5:19).

As Christians, we find ourselves in the midst of a battle on enemy occupied territory, as the world desires us to be conformed to its image (1 Peter 1:14). But God wants us to do what is right by His Word, and renew our minds and actions to be conformed to the will of God (Romans 12:1-2).

Jesus Christ said, "Blessed are: the poor in spirit...those who mourn...the meek...those who hunger and thirst for righteousness...blessed are the merciful...the pure in heart...the peacemakers...those who are persecuted for righteousness' sake...and when they revile and persecute you, and say all kinds of evil against you" (Matthew 5:3-11).

Day 26

Blessed Are Those Who Hunger For God

"Blessed are you poor, for yours is the Kingdom of God. Blessed are you who hunger now, for you shall be filled. Blessed are you who weep now, for you shall laugh. Blessed are you when men hate you and when they exclude you, and revile you and cast out your name as evil for the Son of Man's sake. Rejoice in that day and leap for joy! For indeed your reward is great in heaven, for in like manner their fathers did to the prophets. But woe to you who are rich, for you have received your consolation. Woe to you who are full, for you shall hunger. Woe to you who laugh now, for you shall mourn and weep. Woe to you when all men speak well of you, for so did their fathers to the false prophets" (Luke 6:20-26).

One of the great perils of living in this world, whilst not being of it (1 John 4:4), is the fact we are in danger of being drawn into the ungodly worldview and values of our culture. Some Christians view the godless rich or famous to admire them and get drawn in, and suddenly their pulpits ring with messages drawn from secular worldviews (1 Timothy 4:1).

To be rich, successful, full and jovial without God is a very dangerous thing. All these things – the money, success and the high-spirited mocking laughter all keep people from the Kingdom of God (James 5:1-6). Today, it is the rich, full and laughing nations which are cold towards the gospel; whilst the poor of Africa, Asia and South America etc., are turning to Christ in their millions. In the West millions have no time for God, as they are busy laughing at the TV, filling their bellies with too much food and buying products. This is why Christ confides that the poor are blessed – they will be filled and they will laugh in His eternal Kingdom; whilst the godless rich will be tormented (Luke 16:19-31).

God's heart is not with the rich, wealthy and satisfied, but with the poor and lonely. 'Has God not chosen the poor of this world to be rich in faith and heirs of the Kingdom which He promised to those who love Him?' (James 2:5). Those who are content with their earthly riches without Christ, will be lost forever and God says to them, "Woe! Take heed!"

Day 27

Pass on God's Grace

"It was said, 'You shall love your neighbour and hate your enemy.' But I say to you, love your enemies, bless those who curse you, do good to those who hate you, and pray for those who spitefully use you and persecute you, that you may be sons of your Father in heaven; for He makes His sun rise on the evil and on the good, and sends rain on the just and on the unjust. For if you love those who love you, what reward have you? Do not even the tax collectors do the same? And if you greet your brethren only, what do you do more than others? Do not even the tax collectors do so? Therefore you shall be perfect, just as your Father in heaven is perfect" (Matthew 5:43-48).

Some of the seemingly impossible parts of Jesus' teaching concerns how believers should respond to their enemies. Through this teaching we learn that God's love is stronger than mankind's hatred. After all, it was God who first loved us, whilst we were indifferent to Him at best, or raging against Him in sin. 'We love Him because He first loved us' (1 John 4:19). In the same way God urges believers to show His grace to fellow human beings. It is natural to get angry, seek revenge and to hate, but it is godly to forgive and seek the good of another. The circles of anger and hate, so vivid in the world, can be broken by acts of courageous love.

Christ promised rewards will be given in heaven to those who meet these difficult standards; and also these acts are part of unseen spiritual warfare (Ephesians 6:12). 'If your enemy is hungry, give him bread to eat; and if he is thirsty, give him water to drink. For so you will heap coals of fire on his head and the Lord will reward you' (Proverbs 25:21-22).

The person who seeks revenge, filled with anger and unforgiveness abides outside of God's peace. Thus, we are encouraged to lay down all carnal self-destructive attitudes – "Freely you have received, freely give" (Matthew 10:8).

Jesus reminds us that God's gift of life in nature is given to all. As God is merciful, so must we be; as we wait for all to be put right on Judgment Day. 'Bless those who persecute you; bless and do not curse' (Romans 12:14).

Day 28

God Suffers Us

"You have heard that it was said, 'An eye for an eye and a tooth for a tooth.' But I tell you not to resist an evil person. But whoever slaps you on your right cheek, turn the other to him also. If anyone wants to sue you and take away your tunic, let him have your cloak also. And whoever compels you to go one mile, go with him two. Give to him who asks you and from him who wants to borrow from you do not turn away" (Matthew 5:38-42).

In the Old Testament, a culture of retaliation established as people sought to 'get revenge.' Samson's life was a circle of sin, being sinned against and seeking revenge, leading to much misery (Judges 15:7). Instead of following this pattern, we are told to begin to tolerate wrongs against us and to try to go further each day into grace, to walk the next mile.

Christ wants to stop the poison of revenge destroying our lives and others. In the past we said, "They did it to me and I will do it to them," yet God says, "Do not hold it against them – go further into grace." By suffering any wrong, we do not defend the sin, but release ourselves from daily drinking the poisoned cup of bitterness. By choosing the good, we do not become defined or controlled by what others have done.

This is not a charter for believers to become the victims of bullies, dictators or domestic tyrants. In His Passion, Jesus accepted being struck many times, yet He also challenged them once, asking if it was just, "If I have spoken evil, bear witness of the evil; but if well, why do you strike Me?" (John 18:23). When Paul was struck he asked for justice, "Do you strike me...contrary to the Law" (Acts 23:3). When he was arrested Paul also stressed his legal rights (Acts 22:25).

When we forgive it is a personal matter and we are not permitted to undermine the authority of the police, judges or the law. We cannot release others from the punishment of breaking the law, because we are subjects of the law, not its judge (Romans 13:1-7). The law of the land must run its course, as we follow the law of Christ in the heart. 'Do not be overcome by evil, but overcome evil with good' (Romans 12:21). Violence begets violence, whilst love leads to grace.

Day 29

Do Unto Others

"Therefore, whatever you want men to do to you, do also to them, for this is the Law and the Prophets" (Matthew 7:12).

Jesus explained that the entire Old Testament, all the laws and all the exhortations of the prophets can be summed up in – treat others as you want to be treated. Consequently, before we say something mean, judge another, criticise, get angry, or plan something bad for another…or steal, cheat, lie and swear etc.,…God encourages us to ask ourselves – "How would I like to be on the receiving end of…?"

Would we like to be lied to, cheated, stolen from, judged, hurt and abused, etc.? Christ also explained that this way of life is only possible when we love God first and foremost. Christ said, "You shall love the Lord your God with all your heart, with all your soul, with all your mind and with all your strength.' This is the first commandment. And the second, like it, is this: 'You shall love your neighbour as yourself.' There is no other commandment greater than these" (Mark 12:29-31). Paul concluded: 'All the Law is fulfilled in one word, even in this: "You shall love your neighbour as yourself" ' (Galatians 5:14-15). James called it, 'The Royal Law' of the Scriptures (James 2:8).

It is important to understand God is not asking for us to be fakes, trying to manifest phoney feelings of love for another, but instead to let our actions do our talking. 'Brotherly love,' is what we are commanded to (2 Peter 1:7). This kind of love is expressed by what we do, rather than how we feel. As God extends mercy, grace and forgiveness to us, so we should extend it to others. As God goes the extra mile with us, so must we (Matthew 5:41). As God loves us, even if He does not like our behaviour, so we are to imitate Him.

Accordingly, we have a duty of Christian care to all, and are bound by the principles of Christ's mercy and grace. Before we do anything to another we must ask ourselves: 1. If I was the recipient of…would I like it? 2. Am I prepared to reap what I am sowing? (Galatians 6:7). 3. Will I be pleased with…on Judgment Day? 4. Does this action proceed from selfless Christian love and does it manifest God's grace?

Day 30

When You Pray

"When you pray, do not use vain repetitions as the heathen do, for they think that they will be heard for their many words. Therefore do not be like them. For your Father knows the things you have need of before you ask Him. In this manner, therefore, pray: 'Our Father in heaven, hallowed be Your name. Your Kingdom come, Your will be done, on earth as it is in heaven. Give us this day our daily bread and forgive us our debts, as we forgive our debtors. And do not lead us into temptation, but deliver us from the evil one. For Yours is the Kingdom and the power and the glory forever. Amen.' For if you forgive men their trespasses, your heavenly Father will also forgive you. But if you do not forgive men their trespasses, neither will your Father forgive your trespasses" (Matthew 6:7-15).

Prior to unveiling the Lord's Prayer, it is remarkable that Jesus Christ warns us not to make, "Vain repetitions" and how often have these words been said in empty repetition? Consequently, mindless duplication of prayer has no effect; instead we are to believe and to pray as the Holy Spirit leads (Mark 11:24). 'Likewise the Spirit also helps in our weaknesses. For we do not know what we should pray for as we ought, but the Spirit Himself makes intercession for us with groanings which cannot be uttered. Now He who searches the hearts knows what the mind of the Spirit is, because He makes intercession for the saints according to the will of God' (Romans 8:26-27).

In the Lord's Prayer we are given guidance on how and what to pray. First we are to honour God, "Hallowed be Your name." Then, we are to pray for God's will to be done – in our situation – as we believe for the fulfilment of Christ's Kingdom plans. We must also major on the minors in our lives. What do we need? Is it God's will? Does anything hinder our prayers? Have we forgiven all? If not, we cannot be forgiven and our prayers are in vain! Now, remember we are in a spiritual battle. "But deliver us from the evil one," and finally, we remember who is in charge. "For Yours is the Kingdom and the power and the glory forever. Amen."

Day 31

Keep Asking, Seeking and Knocking

"Which of you shall have a friend and go to him at midnight and say to him, 'Friend, lend me three loaves; for a friend of mine has come to me on his journey and I have nothing to set before him;' and he will answer from within and say, 'Do not trouble me; the door is now shut and my children are with me in bed; I cannot rise and give to you?'

"I say to you, though he will not rise and give to him because he is his friend, yet because of his persistence he will rise and give him as many as he needs. So I say to you, ask and it will be given to you; seek and you will find; knock and it will be opened to you. For everyone who asks receives and he who seeks finds, and to him who knocks it will be opened. If a son asks for bread from any father among you, will he give him a stone? Or if he asks for a fish, will he give him a serpent instead of a fish? Or if he asks for an egg, will he offer him a scorpion? If you then, being evil, know how to give good gifts to your children, how much more will your heavenly Father give the Holy Spirit to those who ask Him!" (Luke 11:5-13).

Through Scripture we learn we are in spiritual battle every time we engage in prayer (Revelation 8:4). Jesus declared, "When you pray," noting the need for "persistence;" to keep on asking, seeking and knocking in prayer. God is good and He wants to bless us with everything we legitimately need. The Lord said, "If you then, being evil, know how to give good gifts to your children, how much more will your Father who is in heaven give good things to those who ask Him!" (Matthew 7:11). God especially notes the gift of His Spirit!

Nevertheless, we are also shown in the Bible that prayers have to find their way through the fog of spiritual battle in the heavenly realms (Ephesians 6:12). There are angels being sent out in battle and evil spiritual forces are fighting them.

An angel said to Daniel, "From the first day...your words were heard and I have come because of your words. But the prince of the Kingdom of Persia (an evil spirit) withstood me twenty-one days; and behold, Michael (a chief archangel of God)...came to help" (Daniel 10:12-13, Revelation 12:7).

Day 32

Is it God's Will?

"Or do you think that I cannot now pray to My Father and He will provide Me with more than twelve legions of angels? How then could the Scriptures be fulfilled, that it must happen thus?" (Matthew 26:53-54).

One of the most important lessons for Christians to learn is that we cannot ask God to fulfil a promise He never made. Far too often Christians plead Scriptures out of context, and without reference to their counterparts and counterbalances in the rest of the Bible (1 Corinthians 14:32, 2 Timothy 3:16). When Jesus was faced with arrest, He knew He could pray and ask for a great multitude of angels to save Him, but He accepted it was not the will of God. The purposes of God the Father, as foretold by the prophets, had to be fulfilled.

Before we ask for anything in prayer, we should first ask ourselves if our petitions are God's will, and have we met the conditions for prayer to be heard and answered? God's faithfulness to answer prayer should never be questioned; His answer may be, "No," or it could be that we ignored His requirements for prayer to be received and answered.

The Bible stresses we can have confidence in prayer being answered when it is according to God's will (1 John 5:14-15). The Lord told us to pray, "Your will be done" (Matthew 6:10), and to pray in 'Jesus' name' means to pray according to His will, for God's glory (John 14:13-14).

Before making requests we must first confess and forsake sin, to pray with clean hands and pure hearts (Psalm 24:4, 66:17-19, Proverbs 28:13, 1 John 3:21-22). All our praying must be unselfish, with holy eternal motives (James 4:3). Any petition grounded in proud worldly ambition does not meet the criteria! The fruitfulness of our prayers is also correlated to us having godly, holy relationships with others (Matthew 5:23-24, 1 Peter 3:7), anchored in Holy Spirit unity (Psalm 133, John 17:20-23). We are right to be persistent in our prayers (Luke 11:5-10, 18:1-8), but obeying this, without regarding all other biblical guides is foolhardy. Trying to pray without heartfelt repentance will always be ineffective. Do we meet the conditions? (2 Chronicles 7:14).

Day 33

Labour For God in All Things

"My Father has been working until now and I have been working" (John 5:17).

One of the contentions the religious leaders had with Jesus was that He healed people on the Sabbath. The Law stated, 'Six days you shall labour and do all your work...but the seventh day is the Sabbath of the Lord your God' (Exodus 20:9). God gave mankind six days to do their work and one for rest and full devotion; despite this the religious leaders tainted this rest, with endless religiosity and rules. Jesus rebuked them saying, "The Sabbath was made for man and not man for the Sabbath" (Mark 2:27).

In the economy of God for our lives, we find a pattern of six days of work and one for resting in God. When Jesus was ministering on earth, He worked very hard. The Lord said, "I must work the works of Him who sent Me while it is day; the night is coming when no one can work" (John 9:4-5).

God created man to work (Genesis 2:5), but the fall marred the joy He planned for our working lives (Genesis 3:17-19). Be that as it may, hard work for both sexes is still praised by God (Proverbs 14:23, 31:27), and those who can, but refuse to work, have by their laziness disqualified themselves from Christian charity (Matthew 25:26, 2 Thessalonians 3:10-12).

As it is God's will for all to work, either in a job, career, ministry, or raising a family etc., our labour should not be considered unholy. Paul wrote in the context of working: 'Whatever you do, do it heartily, as to the Lord and not to men, knowing that from the Lord you will receive the reward of the inheritance; for you serve the Lord Christ' (Colossians 3:23-24). He entreats believers, 'Knowing that whatever good anyone does, he will receive the same from the Lord' (Ephesians 6:8). The principle of sowing to the Lord in our labour and reaping from Him is evident (Galatians 6:7).

With all we earn from our labour we must, 'Provide for our own.' But if we refuse to work and support our families we are, 'Worse than an unbeliever' (1 Timothy 5:8). It is wise to save for future difficulties, to tithe and to help those in need (Genesis 41:34-36, Proverbs 13:22, Ephesians 4:28).

Day 34

Give and it Shall be Given

'Now Jesus sat opposite the treasury and saw how the people put money into the treasury. And many who were rich put in much. Then one poor widow came and threw in two mites, which make a quadrans. So He called His disciples to Himself and said to them, "Assuredly, I say to you that this poor widow has put in more than all those who have given to the treasury; for they all put in out of their abundance, but she out of her poverty put in all that she had, her whole livelihood" ' (Mark 12:41-44).

As our working lives and need for income dominates much of our time, God has lots to say about them. God's plan for our lives is all inclusive and Jesus spoke many times about money. The practice of tithing, which is giving God the first ten percent of our earnings began before the Law (Genesis 14:17-20, Numbers 18:21-32), and into the period of grace.

Giving tithes and offerings to God proves we love Him, as we overcome the spirit of mammon (Luke 16:13). 'Honour the Lord with your possessions and with the firstfruits of all your increase; so your barns will be filled with plenty and your vats will overflow with new wine' (Proverbs 3:9-10).

When Jesus spoke about tithing, He said it should not be left, "Undone" (Luke 11:42). He taught that our giving is not measured by how much we give, but by what it costs us to give. If the Law stated a minimum of ten percent of our income belongs to God, grace calls for more (Romans 5:20), with the prospect of it all being available for God (Romans 12:1). This widow was honored for giving sacrificially, whilst the rich ruler loved money more than God (Luke 18:18-27).

The gospel is free, although sending it costs (1 Corinthians 9:13). 'The Lord has commanded that those who preach the gospel should live from the gospel' (1 Corinthians 9:14). If we value the gospel we will help send it to others (1 Corinthians 16:2), as others did for us, and we will receive rewards (Philippians 4:17); but if we, 'Sow sparingly,' we will 'Reap sparingly' (2 Corinthians 9:6). 'So let each one give as he purposes in his heart, not grudgingly or of necessity; for God loves a cheerful giver' (2 Corinthians 9:7).

Day 35

Secret Faithfulness is Rewarded

"Take heed that you do not do your charitable deeds before men, to be seen by them. Otherwise you have no reward from your Father in heaven. Therefore, when you do a charitable deed, do not sound a trumpet before you as the hypocrites do in the synagogues and in the streets, that they may have glory from men. Assuredly, I say to you, they have their reward. But when you do a charitable deed, do not let your left hand know what your right hand is doing, that your charitable deed may be in secret; and your Father who sees in secret will Himself reward you openly" (Matthew 6:1-4).

There is a reoccurring theme in Jesus' teaching – what we do in secret, will forever be more important than what we do in public. In addition, if we do something good in order to be seen, we will receive no reward from God for that deed.

Christ said, "When you do a charitable deed" – providing us with the principle that giving is part of the Christian life. We are to put self aside and perceive the needs of others in the world, and accept God choosing to use us to help meet other's needs. Nevertheless, we are warned that if we give, pray or fast to be seen by others, we will *not* be rewarded.

What is in our hearts is essential and when our motives are right before God, we will obey Jesus without looking for anyone else's approval or praise. Then, "Your Father who sees in secret will Himself reward you openly."

All we do for Christ should be made manifest to follow the inward principle of obedience to Him – not to try to feed off of people's praise. When we take less notice of ourselves and seek for nothing more than the joy of obeying Christ, God will reward us. This principle of secrecy in obedience is echoed in Jesus' teaching – "When you pray, go into your room and when you have shut your door, pray to your Father who is in the secret place; and your Father who sees in secret will reward you openly...when you fast, anoint your head and wash your face, so that you do not appear to men to be fasting...and your Father who sees in secret will reward you openly" (Matthew 6:6-7, 17-18).

Day 36

Do Not Worry

"Therefore I say to you, do not worry about your life, what you will eat or what you will drink; nor about your body, what you will put on. Is not life more than food and the body more than clothing? Look at the birds of the air, for they neither sow nor reap, nor gather into barns; yet your heavenly Father feeds them. Are you not of more value than they? Which of you by worrying can add one cubit to his stature? So why do you worry about clothing? Consider the lilies of the field, how they grow: they neither toil nor spin; and yet I say to you even Solomon in all his glory was not arrayed like one of these. Now if God so clothes the grass of the field, which today is and tomorrow is thrown into the oven, will He not much more clothe you, O you of little faith?" (Matthew 6:25-30).

The Bible provides much guidance on what we often call the battlefield of the mind. Seven times in the Gospels it documents Jesus saying, "Do not worry." He asks, "Which of you by worrying...?" At some point we must acknowledge worrying does not change our situations; it just robs us of today's peace. The Lord asks, "Is not life more than...?"

The Lord counsels us of the brevity of life and the unreality of much we desire. People are valuable, they are eternal; all else is temporal. Our first and foremost thoughts should be eternal. Jesus said, "Seek first the Kingdom of God and its righteousness." With this foundation in place, we need to trust in God's providence and Lordship over our lives, and needs – as we obey and are wise in all things, including budgeting! The Lord said, "Therefore do not worry about tomorrow, for tomorrow will worry about its own things. Sufficient for the day is its own trouble" (Matthew 6:34).

In this section of practical down to earth advice, Christ tells us to put God first in all and deal with the problems to be solved today, whilst trusting God for tomorrow. Paul wrote: 'Let the peace of God rule in your hearts' (Colossians 3:15). Have you ever considered that endless worrying could be an act of disobedience, as we enthrone fear and doubt above faith in the providence of God? (Philippians 4:19).

Day 37

Gaining the World Means Nothing

"For what will it profit a man if he gains the whole world, and loses his own soul? Or what will a man give in exchange for his soul? For whoever is ashamed of Me and My words in this adulterous and sinful generation, of him the Son of Man also will be ashamed when He comes in the glory of His Father with the holy angels" (Mark 8:36-38).

Jesus Christ described His generation as a, "Adulterous and sinful generation." Surely, things have not become any better. In fact, it is through reading the Bible that we learn how sinful the world is. If we compare our culture to God's described will in the Bible, we discover we too are, "A wicked and adulterous generation" (Matthew 16:4).

The beliefs, values and the culture of Christians should be very different from the world. Jesus said, "I am not of this world" and, "My Kingdom is not of this world" (John 8:23, 18:36). Paul proclaimed, "If then you were raised with Christ, seek those things which are above, where Christ is, sitting at the right hand of God. Set your mind on things above, not on things on the earth" (Colossians 3:1-2).

It is important for believers in Jesus to consent that earth is not our genuine home. We are first and foremost citizens of the Kingdom of God (Philippians 3:20). We are presently on a mission for God, on enemy occupied territory called earth, as the prince of the power of the air continues to deceive the nations to defy God's will (Revelation 20:3). There are fallen angels battling, who work in and through the sons of disobedience (Ephesians 2:2); and if we are not careful, we too can be deceived by the web of the enemy (Mark 13:22).

With this in mind, the next time we hear of the world's richest person or greatest star, or if we find ourselves trying to keep up with the Jones' with our possessions or opinions, remember the fallen angel named Satan is trying to deceive. Christ urges us to perceive reality – it all means nothing eternally. What have they gained if they lose their souls to hell? Can they exchange their money or fame for salvation? If we live for eighty years, we have just over 29,000 days on earth; then the judgment and real life or death begins!

Day 38

What Did You Go Out To See?

'When the messengers of John had departed, He began to speak to the multitudes concerning John, "What did you go out into the wilderness to see? A reed shaken by the wind? But what did you go out to see? A man clothed in soft garments? Indeed those who are gorgeously apparelled and live in luxury are in kings' courts. But what did you go out to see? A prophet? Yes, I say to you and more than a prophet. This is he of whom it is written: 'Behold, I send My messenger before Your face, who will prepare Your way before You.' For I say to you, among those born of women there is not a greater prophet than John the Baptist; but he who is least in the Kingdom of God is greater than he" (Luke 7:24-28).

In this exhortation the Lord provides a comparison between the reality of this fallen broken deceived world (1 John 5:19), and God's plan being outworked on earth. In the palaces of Herod Antipas (the ruler of Galilee in Jesus' time), were people "gorgeously apparelled" and living in luxury. The devil, who is at work in every age had kept them blinded to the fact that the Creator was amongst them (2 Corinthians 4:4), who came to seek and save the lost (Luke 19:10).

These people believed they had power – living as rulers in the Roman Empire and they were deceived, unable to see eternal reality (Titus 3:3). They began to believe their own press, just as we do today. They forgot that civilisations, cultures, structures of power and empires are temporal. "Man who is born of woman is of few days and full of trouble. He comes forth like a flower and fades away; he flees like a shadow and does not continue" (Job 14:1-2).

Since Christ's day countless numbers have lived and died, most are forgotten; few are remembered. All they fought lived and died for, is as nothing to them now. They are either with Christ or in torment (Luke 12:5). We also are playing the same foolish power games like the Romans once did. We are building our 'empires,' seeking more and lusting for recognition. What is Jesus' remedy? Don't pursue what the world wants, seek first God's Kingdom (Matthew 6:33).

Day 39

What Are You Seeking?

"Do not seek what you should eat or what you should drink, nor have an anxious mind. For all these things the nations of the world seek after and your Father knows that you need these things. But seek the Kingdom of God and all these things shall be added to you" (Luke 12:29-31).

If you want a trip to shake you out of spiritual complacency and wake yourself up to eternal realties – take a trip to the rubbish/trash tip and scrap yard! Go and look at the rusting cars, the old mobile phones, the rotten clothes, the spoiled food and smell the stench (Matthew 6:19). After you have grasped the waste products of our civilisation, remind yourself that one, ten or twenty years ago people were working overtime, fighting competitors, battling and queuing to obtain that 'trash.' Many gave up their marriages, missed watching their children grow-up, had no time to spend with God in prayer or to read the Bible – all so they could own their vanity goods (James 5:1-3). I own, therefore I am!

Christ urges us to wake up from our spiritual slumber, to learn what is vain and what valuable. In this age, people will sleep on the streets and pay over the odds to be the first to have a new smart phone, just because of its expensive brand. But soon it is old, out-of-date and has lost much of its value. What then did these people queue for? It was not the phone, but the appearance of status.

Jesus advocates finding an eternal perspective; "For after all these things the Gentiles seek." Their passions are temporary and many are giving up much now, to obtain what will soon be considered rubbish. Jesus said, "But seek first the Kingdom of God and His righteousness, and all these things shall be added to you" (Matthew 6:33). God knows we need livelihoods and there are necessities in life which cannot be avoided, yet on Judgment Day will our spending appear futile or eternally wise? Bibles for China or a new...?

In the days of John the Baptist many leaders were dressed luxuriously, living in palaces, whilst John lived in a desert. We still praise those living in luxury, but God's man was John, who now lives in a heavenly mansion (John 14:2).

Day 40

If, If, If and But

"Therefore if you bring your gift (Matthew 5:23)...For if you love those who love you, what reward have you? (Matthew 5:46)...For if you forgive men their trespasses, your heavenly Father will also forgive you (Matthew 6:15)...Again I say to you that if two of you agree..." (Matthew 18:19).

Christians have often been in danger of trying to claim the results of obedience, whilst choosing to live in perpetual disobedience (James 1:22). To become wise, it is important for every Christian to know, understand and apply the 'ifs' and 'buts' of the Bible. God often says to us, "If you do this, I will do that," and adds, "But if you do not, I will not."

All believers are subject to the terms and conditions of Jesus' new covenant (Matthew 26:28, 2 Corinthians 3:6). In our culture we do not appreciate how important a covenant was in biblical days; the closest we come to it is found in a legally binding agreement. For example, if you have signed a contract with your employer, it explains the benefits of working for them and the conditions to receive the benefits. If you do not turn up for work, you will not get paid. If you publish confidential information, you could get taken to court and punished, etc.

A covenant is a Divine binding agreement between God and man, administered by God and it will form the basis of the terms and conditions which will be applied on Judgment Day. When we confessed faith in Christ Jesus, we verbally accepted an agreement with God in the spiritual realm. One stipulation of this agreement or covenant states: 'If you confess with your mouth the Lord Jesus and believe in your heart that God has raised Him from the dead, you will be saved' (Romans 10:9). God holds us to His covenant and this is why we are given a warning. 'Of how much worse punishment, do you suppose, will he be thought worthy who has trampled the Son of God underfoot, counted the blood of the covenant by which he was sanctified a common thing and insulted the Spirit of grace? For we know Him who said, "Vengeance is Mine, I will repay," says the Lord. And again, "The Lord will judge His people" ' (Hebrews 10:29-30).

Day 41

Terms and Conditions Apply

"For the Son of Man will come in the glory of His Father with His angels and then He will reward each according to his works" (Matthew 16:27).

A biblical covenant is a spiritual agreement between God and His people, in which God makes certain promises and requires certain obedience's from them in return.

In the covenant God made with Moses and Israel, there were many terms and conditions which God's people did not meet; so Christ came to fulfil all the conditions, in order for us to be saved by faith (Hebrews 8:8-13, 10:38). Jesus said, "For this is My blood of the new covenant, which is shed for many for the remission of sins" (Matthew 26:28-29).

Christ's salvation is a free gift. 'For if the blood of bulls and goats and the ashes of a heifer, sprinkling the unclean, sanctifies for the purifying of the flesh, how much more shall the blood of Christ, who through the eternal Spirit offered Himself without spot to God, cleanse your conscience from dead works to serve the living God? And for this reason He is the Mediator of the new covenant, by means of death, for the redemption of the transgressions under the first covenant, that those who are called may receive the promise of the eternal inheritance' (Hebrews 9:13-15).

Christ's new covenant has wonderful certainty (Hebrews 12:24); we have confidence because God has promised and is faithful. Now we must ask – are we faithful? In the terms and conditions of the new covenant, we find what God expects of us, and what we will receive in return. God, the unchanging One, gives us an offer – "I'll do this, if you do that..." e.g., "Confess, repent and I will forgive" etc.

The terms and conditions of the new covenant are found in the Bible. Some are basic standards to prove we are saved (James 2:26), others come with rewards. Salvation is free (Ephesians 2:8), whilst many rewards are conditional on what we do. "For whoever gives you a cup of water to drink in My name, because you belong to Christ, assuredly, I say to you he will by no means lose his reward" (Mark 9:41). Jesus Christ will, "Reward each according to his works."

Day 42

God's Promises are Conditional

"Moreover, when you fast, do not be like the hypocrites, with a sad countenance. For they disfigure their faces that they may appear to men to be fasting. Assuredly, I say to you, they have their reward. But you, when you fast, anoint your head and wash your face, so that you do not appear to men to be fasting, but to your Father who is in the secret place; and your Father who sees in secret will reward you openly" (Matthew 6:16-18).

Frequently believers in Jesus are discouraged when their prayers are not answered, or when things do not turn out as they hoped. Some begin to doubt God's faithfulness, but perhaps we should question ourselves first. Have we met the biblical terms and conditions to receive? What if we had fasted for revival, but failed to heed Christ's teaching, as we boasted in our fast, whilst also failing to meet the terms of 2 Chronicles 7:14? Who would be in the wrong, God or us?

Most of the promises in the Bible are conditional, as God says to us, "I'll do this, if you do that." If we do not meet the conditions God's sets to claim His promises, then we have no reason to make a claim or to moan afterwards.

The granting of God's promises to His people does not depend upon our feelings or circumstances; rather it is upon our fulfilling the terms and conditions God designates in Scripture. This demonstrates the need for us to be diligent to search for, learn and apply the conditions God openly reveals in the Bible (Romans 10:6-9). Remember, Jesus explained that all His disciples must be taught, "To observe all things that I have commanded you" (Matthew 28:20).

Once again, we must accept we never need to, nor can we work for our free gift of salvation (Romans 5:15, Ephesians 2:8). Instead we must continue in our labour of love, in obedience to the Spirit, for the glorification of Jesus. 'For God is not unjust to forget your work and labour of love which you have shown toward His name, in that you have ministered to the saints, and do minister' (Hebrews 6:10).

"You are My friends if you do whatever I command you," said Jesus (John 15:14). Do we obey the 'Ifs' of the Bible?

Day 43

Contrary to the World

"Enter by the narrow gate; for wide is the gate and broad is the way that leads to destruction and there are many who go in by it. Because narrow is the gate and difficult is the way which leads to life, and there are few who find it. Beware of false prophets, who come to you in sheep's clothing, but inwardly they are ravenous wolves. You will know them by their fruits. Do men gather grapes from thornbushes or figs from thistles? Even so, every good tree bears good fruit, but a bad tree bears bad fruit. A good tree cannot bear bad fruit, nor can a bad tree bear good fruit. Every tree that does not bear good fruit is cut down and thrown into the fire. Therefore by their fruits you will know them" (Matthew 7:13-20).

One of the reasons pick-n-mix spirituality has become popular for some in the West is because they perceive a spirituality which costs them little. They believe they can live as they choose and receive the 'blessings' of being 'spiritual.' But what fruit do we see in their lives?

Most people in the world are going with the flow, following the crowd and offer no resistance to the stream. Disciples of Jesus Christ are not permitted to do this. We have to stand apart, be strong and walk in the opposite direction. We are told that many are on a road which leads to destruction and one by one millions are walking towards an eternal cliff. This road is filled with all kinds of broken pleasures of sin and much temporal amusement; its end is death. We are exhorted to seek out and walk through, "The narrow gate."

The way into the eternal Kingdom is narrow and difficult, so don't be surprised when you find your values in conflict with the world. We are not of this world (John 16:33).

Jesus said, "If the world hates you, you know that it hated Me before it hated you. If you were of the world, the world would love its own. Yet because you are not of the world, but I chose you out of the world, therefore the world hates you. Remember the Word that I said to you, 'A servant is not greater than his master.' If they persecuted Me, they will also persecute you" (John 15:18-20).

Day 44

Jesus and Government

"My Kingdom is not of this world" (John 18:36).

One intriguing aspect of Jesus Christ's life is how little He esteemed temporal politics. He did not come to redeem the Roman Empire or to put right its wrongs; instead He came to establish an eternal Kingdom (Luke 4:43).

As a child, Jesus was made a refugee and forced to flee His dictatorial government. After returning to Judea, He grew living under brutal Roman occupation. But, when the centurion's servant was sick years later, Jesus did not make political demands; instead He healed as a testimony of God (Luke 7:1-10). Many Jews sought an occasion for an uprising, whilst Jesus taught, "Render therefore to Caesar the things that are Caesar's and to God the things that are God's" (Luke 20:25). Only John said what repentance would mean for Roman soldiers, "Do not intimidate anyone or accuse falsely and be content with your wages" (Luke 3:14).

Politics forever changes, but Christ's demands on our lives are eternal. We are told by Jesus to meet the requirements of government and God. Paul wrote we must be subject, pay taxes, obey godly law and do good (Romans 13:1-7). Only when God's will and the authorities came into conflict did the apostles say, "We ought to obey God rather than men" (Acts 5:29). Paul knew Daniel's prophecy, "The God of heaven will set up a Kingdom which shall never be destroyed..." (Daniel 2:44). He lived with the eternal Kingdom in mind and spoke of eternity to government (Acts 24:10-21). Jesus' and Paul's teaching are amazing, considering both knew they would be prisoners and die under Roman rule (Luke 9:22, Acts 9:16).

In Jesus' day, tax collectors were despised collaborators, yet the Lord's care for Zacchaeus led to his repentance and salvation (Luke 19:1-10). This tax collector's penitent heart was revealed, when he said, "Look, Lord, I give half of my goods to the poor and if I have taken anything from anyone by false accusation, I restore fourfold." Jesus said, "Today salvation has come to this house, because he also is a son of Abraham; for the Son of Man has come to seek and to save that which was lost" (Luke 19:8-10).

Day 45

Judge Yourself Only

"Judge not, that you be not judged. For with what judgment you judge, you will be judged; and with the measure you use, it will be measured back to you. And why do you look at the speck in your brother's eye, but do not consider the plank in your own eye?" (Matthew 7:1-3).

Christ did not save believers so they could sit in His seat as judges, to tear apart others (Galatians 5:15). He warns all to examine their own spiritual lives and make sure they are faithfully walking in Him. Paul wrote: 'Examine yourselves as to whether you are in the faith. Test yourselves. Do you not know yourselves, that Jesus Christ is in you? – unless indeed you are disqualified' (2 Corinthians 13:5).

God urges us not to focus on others, but to examine our own hearts, actions and beliefs. He wants us to invite the Holy Spirit to purify our hearts, to make us more like Christ. If we spend our time judging others we will become spiritually stagnant, due to our disobedience. We can never know the full facts to judge fairly, therefore we must not. James warns those who judge others without authority are trying to sit as a judge in Christ's place (James 4:11-12).

Christian leaders and prophets have appropriate authority to judge under Christ, for edification (1 Corinthians 6:4), and to expose falsehoods (Matthew 13:36-43), but this does not permit spiteful personal judgments of others in the flesh.

Satan is, 'The accuser of our brethren, who accused them before our God day and night' (Revelation 12:10). His desire is to tear apart the body of Christ (John 17:15), which Jesus prayed would be one (John 17:21); and when we judge, we are joining in the condemnation and accusation of brethren.

If you want to know what a miserable Christian looks like, find one who spends all his or her time judging others. By doing so, he or she is siding with the accuser of the brethren and will be poisoned in the spirit. We are told to put, 'Evil speaking away' and, 'Be kind, tender hearted, forgiving' otherwise we grieve the Holy Spirit (Ephesians 4:30-32). We must stop trying to fix everyone else, put away our fake heresy hunter title and let the righteous Judge do His work.

Day 46

The Measure of Judgment

'Peter said, "But Lord, what about this man?" Jesus said to him, "If I will that he remain till I come, what is that to you? You follow Me" ' (John 21:21-22).

When Peter wanted to know the fate of John, Jesus said, "What is that to you? You follow Me." Our attitude needs to be the same. 'Who are you to judge another's servant? To his own master he stands or falls' (Romans 14:4).

Jesus illustrated that one of the roles of the Holy Spirit is to convict people of sin (John 16:8), and God forbids believers to judge others in the flesh, as it is sin to set ourselves as a judge in Christ's place (Romans 2:3, James 4:11-12). On the Day of Judgment, it is Christ who will judge everyone by the secrets of their own hearts (Romans 2:16).

Jesus also instructed that if we choose to judge another, "With the measure you use, it will be measured back to you!" Therefore, if we are harsh, cruel and show no mercy to others, we are setting ourselves up for a harsher judgment! Consequently, instead of judging, we are to be merciful. 'For judgment is without mercy to the one who has shown no mercy. Mercy triumphs over judgment' (James 2:13).

Christians are not permitted to judge others in personal vengeance, instead we are told to find the faults in our own lives and change. Nevertheless, Christian leaders, parents, prophets and those in authority do have a responsibility to make holy judgments in church and family situations, etc., as guided by the Bible and the Holy Spirit (1 Corinthians 6:2). This type of assessment proceeds to protect the church or family etc., not to be critics for the sake of it. Those who exercise judgment in churches, teaching others what is God's will, must be cautious, because they will receive a stricter judgment (James 3:1).

By nature we love to judge others, this is why we need to submit to Christ, deny the old man and allow His new nature to be manifested through us (2 Corinthians 5:17). "If anyone desires to come after Me, let him deny himself, and take up his cross and follow Me" (Matthew 16:24). The Church has been called to love the world, not to judge it in the flesh.

Day 47

Live for Eternity

"Woe to you, Bethsaida! For if the mighty works which were done in you had been done in Tyre and Sidon, they would have repented long ago in sackcloth and ashes. But, I say to you, it will be more tolerable for Tyre and Sidon in the Day of Judgment than for you. And you, Capernaum, who are exalted to heaven, will be brought down to Hades; for if the mighty works which were done in you had been done in Sodom, it would have remained until this day. But I say to you that it shall be more tolerable for the land of Sodom in the Day of Judgment than for you" (Matthew 11:21-24).

When the Nazis were in power during WWII, every German soldier felt pressurised to conform to the will and standards of Hitler. Those who opposed or rejected the Nazi worldview were silenced, leading to others being coerced to be quiet or suffer the consequences. Meanwhile, many Nazis embraced the ideology fully and were praised for doing so.

After Germany lost the war, those who had revelled in the Nazi worldview and ideology were exposed to another set of values completely opposite to their own. In the Nuremberg Trials of 1945-46, these criminals were forced to see what they had done in the light of a far wider body of opinion. Once these Nazis had been sheltered in their own worldview and ideology, but suddenly they were exposed to the values of the wider world and they saw themselves in shame.

Why does this matter to us? Because we now live in a culture of accepted sin (Isaiah 5:20), which aborts millions of children, encourages the young into promiscuity, and defies all the cherished values and morals God esteems. Too many 'Christians' feel comfortable in our culture and are not troubled by the sin, as Lot was (2 Peter 2:7). But one day, the curtain on this world will be pulled back and we will witness ourselves from heaven's point of view. Millions of angels and saints will look at us and wonder!

Jesus tells us to focus on eternity and prepare for the Day of Judgment. Far too much teaching in churches today puts an emphasis on this temporal life – getting something, being better, going higher etc., but was this Jesus' teaching?

Day 48

A Detailed Judgment

"I say to you that for every idle word men may speak, they will give account of it in the Day of Judgment. For by your words you will be justified and by your words you will be condemned" (Matthew 12:36-37).

In this passage, Jesus outlines precise details concerning Judgment Day. Christ will weigh all we have said and done, including idle words. These integral ingredients will be called upon in the judgment and they provide us with a warning that God is looking at us every second of every day. There is nothing unseen to Him. 'And there is no creature hidden from His sight, but all things are naked and open to the eyes of Him to whom we must give account' (Hebrews 4:13). But we will be justified by our confession of faith in Jesus.

In the cases of the judgment of the cities of Chorazin, Bethsaida and Capernaum (Luke 10:12-15), Christ explains that what we know of Him and have seen of His works, will play an important part in judgment. "For if the mighty works which were done in you had been done in Tyre and Sidon, they would have repented long ago, sitting in sackcloth and ashes" (Luke 10:13). Therefore, those who know of God, or have seen Him at work will be held to account to a far higher standard than others. "For everyone to whom much is given, from him much will be required; and to whom much has been committed, of him they will ask the more" (Luke 12:48).

Many Christians, subject to poor or bad teaching, rarely hear of the Day of Judgment. The Bible warns there will be false teachers, who do not know the Lord, who will pervert the gospel (1 John 2:19). Also, there will be 'nice' people with bad teaching. On Judgment Day all will be revealed!

What must we do? Obey God in all things, bear in mind He is ever watching as a loving Father and confess all sin to Him. If we do this, we can have confidence. 'Love has been perfected among us in this: that we may have boldness in the Day of Judgment; because as He is, so are we in this world. There is no fear in love; but perfect love casts out fear, because fear involves torment. But he who fears has not been made perfect in love' (1 John 4:17-18).

Day 49

Rash Promises and Foolish Oaths

"Again you have heard that it was said to those of old, 'You shall not swear falsely, but shall perform your oaths to the Lord.' But I say to you, do not swear at all: neither by heaven, for it is God's throne; nor by the earth, for it is His footstool; nor by Jerusalem, for it is the city of the great King. Nor shall you swear by your head because you cannot make one hair white or black. But let your 'Yes' be 'Yes,' and your 'No,' 'No.' For whatever is more than these is from the evil one" (Matthew 5:33-37).

In today's society we treat words and promises very cheaply, but this is not so with God (Numbers 23:19). The Lord takes everything we say seriously and He urges us not to make any promises without counting the cost (Luke 14:28). Jesus said, "For by your words you will be justified and by your words you will be condemned" (Matthew 12:37).

In Bible days, oaths were made as solemn statements to seal treaties, do business and to confirm faithfulness to God etc., (Deuteronomy 27:11-28:68). To make an oath and to break it was a terrible sin before God. Solomon said, "Better not to vow than to vow and not pay" (Ecclesiastes 5:5).

Jesus tells us, "Do not swear at all," but rather, "Let your 'Yes' be 'Yes,' and your 'No,' 'No.' " We must be careful not to make rash promises to God, especially in religious meetings, to dedicate things to Him without carefully weighing the cost. Instead, we should make good choices in our hearts and follow it through daily, without making vows.

James warns us of the dangers of making vows and how they will impact our appraisals on Judgment Day. 'But above all, my brethren, do not swear, either by heaven or by earth or with any other oath. But let your "Yes" be "Yes," and your "No," "No," lest you fall into judgment' (James 5:12).

People should be able to trust the words and promises of believers, and this can only be possible if we do not make rash promises which we cannot keep, or have no control over. But before God, instead of making wild promises and vows, we should give Him all we are daily. Our love is proved, not in word, but by our actions (John 14:15).

Day 50

You are the Church

"For where two or three are gathered together in My name, I am there in the midst of them" (Matthew 18:20).

One of the fundamental distortions of biblical phraseology occurs when Christians say, "We are going to church." When people go to a building called a 'church,' they set aside perhaps one hour a week to be religious. But this concept is not biblical, nor does it demonstrate God's will.

Believers cannot go to 'church,' they are the Church. They are members of the body of Christ (1 Corinthians 12:12-31). Peter teaches us, 'You also, as living stones, are being built up a spiritual house, a holy priesthood, to offer up spiritual sacrifices acceptable to God through Jesus Christ' (1 Peter 2:5). God is not seeking physical buildings to be His home, rather, people who will be living temples of His Holy Spirit.

Stephen taught, 'The Most High does not dwell in temples made with hands' (Acts 7:48), and Paul preached, 'God, who made the world and everything in it, since He is Lord of heaven and earth, does not dwell in temples made with hands' (Acts 17:24). Believers can build buildings, but God will not live there, because God has already told us what His temples are – our bodies (2 Corinthians 6:16).

Jesus testified, ' "If anyone thirsts, let him come to Me and drink. He who believes in Me, as the Scripture has said, out of his heart will flow rivers of living water." But this He spoke concerning the Spirit, whom those believing in Him would receive; for the Holy Spirit was not yet given, because Jesus was not yet glorified' (John 7:37-39).

Our physical bodies have been given a tremendous honour by God. He designed them to be His dwelling place. 'Your body is the temple of the Holy Spirit' (1 Corinthians 6:19). As a result, when two believers meet together to pray and honour Jesus, they are convening in part, a meeting of the body of Christ. They are not going to church, they are being the Church; and when they meet with many others of a like mind, they are together God's temples and Christ is present, in the Person of the Holy Spirit (2 Corinthians 3:17). With the Holy Spirit, everyday is God's holy day (John 15:4).

Day 51

Set Apart

"You are the salt of the earth; but if the salt loses its flavour, how shall it be seasoned? It is then good for nothing but to be thrown out and trampled underfoot by men. You are the light of the world. A city that is set on a hill cannot be hidden. Nor do they light a lamp and put it under a basket, but on a lampstand, and it gives light to all who are in the house. Let your light so shine before men, that they may see your good works and glorify your Father in heaven" (Matthew 5:13-16).

Believers in Jesus Christ are called to be holy and their lifestyles should be distinct from others. When demons were confronted by Jesus they cried out, "Let us alone! What have we to do with You, Jesus of Nazareth? Did You come to destroy us? I know who You are – the Holy One of God!" (Mark 1:24). In the Song of Moses it states: 'Who is like You, O Lord among the gods? Who is like You, glorious in holiness, fearful in praises, doing wonders? (Exodus 15:11). The Hebrew word for 'holy' denotes that which is 'sanctified' or 'set apart.' Believers in Jesus Christ should be both – we are sanctified by faith in Christ's sacrifice (Hebrews 10:10), and set apart for Him. 'But know that the Lord has set apart for Himself him who is godly' (Psalm 4:3).

Jesus points to the fact Christians should be salt and light in the world. In Bible days, salt was used as a preservative, it gave flavour to food (Job 6:6), was linked to health and purity (Ezekiel 16:4), and was used in sacrifices (Ezekiel 43:24). If salt failed in its most basic purpose, it became worthless. If Christians are not different from the world, if we are not salt or light, we too are not fulfilling our purpose. What is the point of hidden light or diluted spoiled salt?

John wrote: 'Do not love the world or the things in the world. If anyone loves the world, the love of the Father is not in him. For all that is in the world – the lust of the flesh, the lust of the eyes and the pride of life – is not of the Father but is of the world. And the world is passing away, and the lust of it; but he who does the will of God abides forever (1 John 2:15-17). Does your life bring God's light to the world?

Day 52

God on a Cross

'He began to teach them that the Son of Man must suffer many things, and be rejected by the elders and chief priests and scribes, and be killed and after three days rise again. He spoke this word openly' (Mark 8:31-32).

The veracity of personal faith is confirmed by our actions, not just our confessions. 'For as the body without the spirit is dead, so faith without works is dead also' (James 2:26). What we do confirms all we accept in our hearts. What we say can be merely vague statements of possible intent. We believe a great many things which have no impact upon our lives, so the validity of our 'beliefs' are tested by our actions.

What kind of belief do we really have in Jesus, if we don't have any time to heed all He said? The Lord told His disciples a time of suffering was ahead for Him, but they did not want to hear it; yet later they accepted it and moved on.

True belief, that is Holy Spirit inspired belief in our hearts, will lead to total transformations in our lives. If we do believe that God died on a cross and rose again on the third day, we will have to sign up to the entire package of His teaching; from the need to be born again, to the explanation of what a God-filled life will mean, and to His teaching on the end times and Judgment Day. It is foolhardy and a product of self-deception to make an open statement of faith in Christ, and then to choose to remain ignorant of what He said, and resist following His commands. 'But be doers of the Word and not hearers only, deceiving yourselves' (James 1:22).

One day, each of us will pass through the veil from which none returns. Our bodies, once so vibrant will fade into the dust, whilst our spirits will live on, either in heaven or hell. Are we preparing for this transition into the world of Christ and God? Too many people do not believe in heaven and hell as real places, just as real as England or the USA. If we all did, we would prepare thoroughly for our transit to the new world. When the first settlers prepared to travel to North America from England, everything they did was in preparation for the journey and new life in the new world. We all make a journey to a new world – are you ready?

Day 53

Treasure in a Field

"The Kingdom of Heaven is like treasure hidden in a field, which a man found and hid; and for joy over it he goes and sells all that he has and buys that field. Again, the Kingdom of Heaven is like a merchant seeking beautiful pearls, who, when he had found one pearl of great price, went and sold all that he had and bought it" (Matthew 13:44-46).

In these two short parables the Lord opens our hearts and minds to the surety of the Kingdom of Heaven. When we find God, it is worth selling all we are and have, to gain Him. Christ is the eternal treasure; He is the unfailing investment, which produces dividends in this life and the next. 'The Kingdom of God is...righteousness and peace and joy in the Holy Spirit' (Romans 14:17). Jesus said, "Assuredly, I say to you, there is no one who has left house or parents or brothers or wife or children, for the sake of the Kingdom of God, who shall not receive many times more in this present time and in the age to come eternal life" (Luke 18:29-30).

Through Jesus' direction, we observe there is more hope, joy and peace inside of God's will, than in everything the world has to offer. The world offers us compromise leading to short-term gain, but Christ tells us to make sacrifices, with rewards in this present age and in the age to come.

Deep inside we all seek contentment and happiness, and in this quest we project our longings onto seeking better careers, relationships, positions of power, titles and express it through religious ambition. But Christ compels us to lay all at His feet and to find the genuine treasure in Him.

Selling-out to Christ does not mean abandoning all sense and responsibility, but to give all to Him, and to allow God to use all we have as He wills. Then, we must follow the Spirit of God, as He leads us into a life of stewardship, rather than ownership. Therefore, when we follow God, we may not have all which the world loves, (which we thought would bring us contentment), but we will have the Prince of Peace and the Spirit of Peace. As Paul testified: 'As poor, yet making many rich; as having nothing and yet possessing all things' (2 Corinthians 6:10).

Day 54

Self-Inflicted Harm

"See, you have been made well. Sin no more, lest a worse thing come upon you" (John 5:14).

It has been estimated that more than ninety percent of all the pain experienced on earth is manmade. This includes all the suffering we inflict on others and all the sinful selfishness which leads to poverty, excess, pollution and misery. Sin has a threefold effect – first it offends God and separates us from Him, second it hurts us, and third it hurts others.

Sin is breaking God's commandments to our own harm. Jesus commands us not to sin because it offends God when His creatures rebel, and second it hurts His creatures when they break His spiritual laws. If we drink the poison of sin, we will feel loathful. 'God is not mocked; for whatever a man sows, that he will also reap' (Galatians 6:7). "With the same measure you use, it will be measured to you" (Mark 4:24).

If we viewed sin from heaven's vantage point, we would never want to abide in sin again, as we witnessed how it disfigures us and others. As every human being is created in the image of God (Genesis 1:26), when we sin against another human, we offend God – his or her Creator.

Sin is so terrible, it leads to death (Romans 6:23); yet God offers forgiveness if we are truly repentant. However, if we are still seeking an excuse to abide in sin, whilst thinking forgiveness can be easily obtained, we will not find it.

On the contrary, if we desire with all our hearts to live holy, and we commit sin and confess it, forgiveness will flow quickly. In fact, when we seek first the Kingdom of God and its righteousness, we will be living in the continual flow of the river of God's grace. 'Of His fullness we have all received and grace for grace. For the Law was given through Moses, but grace and truth came through Jesus Christ' (John 1:16-18). Experiencing God's grace does not lead to taking sin lightly; instead it births life transforming repentance. 'The goodness of God leads you to repentance' (Romans 2:4). 'What then? Shall we sin because we are not under Law but under grace? Certainly not!' (Romans 6:15).

Day 55

Wronging Our Own Souls

"If God were your Father, you would love Me, for I proceeded forth and came from God; nor have I come of Myself, but He sent Me. Why do you not understand My speech? Because you are not able to listen to My Word. You are of your father the devil and the desires of your father you want to do. He was a murderer from the beginning and does not stand in the truth, because there is no truth in him. When he speaks a lie, he speaks from his own resources, for he is a liar and the father of it" (John 8:42-45).

Sin is self-destructive and its end is spiritual and eternal death. 'For the wages of sin is death, but the gift of God is eternal life in Christ Jesus our Lord' (Romans 6:23).

Imagine a man sunk down into the mire of sin; his mouth is filled with expletives and every relationship is broken. He is addicted to alcohol and captivated by bitterness, hatred and spite. What a dark place to be in and yet once this man was an innocent child – created in the image of God. How did this change take place? It was sin which destroyed him.

Satan was the first sinner (1 John 3:8), and his desire is for all to get bogged down into the mire of sin, as he is, to hurt ourselves, others and God. Satan is the liar – the father of all lies; he is the murderer of the souls of mankind and there is no truth in him. Satan is the thief of the soul. Jesus said, "The thief does not come except to steal and to kill, and to destroy. I have come that they may have life and that they may have it more abundantly" (John 10:10).

Why does Satan want all to embrace sin? Because it hurts us, others and is offensive to God. Christ came to break the cycle of sin and give us spiritual abundance. The Spirit of Wisdom (Exodus 28:3, Deuteronomy 34:9, Isaiah 11:2, Ephesians 1:17), provides us with many great lessons and warnings. "Blessed is the man who listens to me, watching daily at my gates, waiting at the posts of my doors. For whoever finds me finds life and obtains favour from the Lord. But he who sins against me wrongs his own soul; all those who hate me love death" (Proverbs 8:34-36).

Day 56

Sin Leads To Suffering

'Jesus said to those Jews, "If you abide in My Word, you are My disciples indeed. And you shall know the truth, and the truth shall make you free." They answered, "We are Abraham's descendants and have never been in bondage to anyone. How can You say, 'You will be made free?' " Jesus answered, "Most assuredly, I say to you, whoever commits sin is a slave of sin. And a slave does not abide in the house forever, but a son abides forever. Therefore if the Son makes you free, you shall be free indeed" ' (John 8:31-36).

There is a momentous deception which many Christians often fall for. This illusion is that some sins are good and we are missing out by avoiding them. Jesus identified Satan as the father of all lies (John 8:45), the one who comes with the intent to, "Kill, steal and destroy" (John 10:10). Sin always comes at a cost, as it causes spiritual slavery and broken lives. How many have been hurt by sexual sin? How many friendships have been broken by foolish anger? How many will be deceived by inner pride? And so it goes on and on.

God created the world observing it as, "Good" (Genesis 1:31), and the first thing Satan wanted to do, was to defy the perfect blueprint God set for Adam and Eve to enjoy fulfilled lives (Genesis 3:1). God placed the first humans in a perfect world, but their sin led to them being cast out into a newly fallen creation, broken and damaged by sin (Genesis 3:24). As stewards of the planet, Adam and Eve's sin also led to massive upheaval in the natural world (Romans 8:20).

Next their offspring began to fight, hate and envy. The first time the word sin is used in the Bible is in Genesis 4:7. God said to Cain, "If you do well, will you not be accepted? And if you do not do well, sin lies at the door. And its desire is for you, but you should rule over it." Cain did not listen, murder was the result and, 'Cain went out from the presence of the Lord' (Genesis 4:11). The second time sin is mentioned is in Genesis 13:13. 'But the men of Sodom were exceedingly wicked and sinful against the Lord.' Here we find the pattern – we sin, it destroys us, we destroy each other and we must leave God's presence, as our sin is an offence to the Lord.

Day 57

Sins of the Heart

"You have heard that it was said to those of old, 'You shall not murder and whoever murders will be in danger of the judgment.' But I say to you that whoever is angry with his brother without a cause shall be in danger of the judgment. And whoever says to his brother, 'Raca!' shall be in danger of the council. But whoever says, 'You fool!' shall be in danger of hell fire. Therefore if you bring your gift to the altar and there remember that your brother has something against you, leave your gift there before the altar, and go your way. First be reconciled to your brother, and then come and offer your gift. Agree with your adversary quickly, while you are on the way with him, lest your adversary deliver you to the judge, the judge hand you over to the officer and you be thrown into prison. Assuredly, I say to you, you will by no means get out of there till you have paid the last penny" (Matthew 5:21-26).

Sin is breaking God's Law (1 John 3:4), either by doing what He forbids or by omitting to do what He commands (Romans 7:9). Before we commit a sin, we often think about it in our hearts, are tempted by it and then commit the sin. James elaborates: 'But each one is tempted when he is drawn away by his own desires and enticed. Then, when desire has conceived, it gives birth to sin; and sin, when it is full-grown, brings forth death' (James 1:14-15).

Under the Old Testament Law, the sin of breaking the Law was judged after the offence; but Jesus refined the matter, condemning the birthing of sin in our hearts. He explains all lust and greed begins in the heart (Mark 7:21). If we allow hate or pride etc., to remain, it will grow leading to more sin.

Christ expounds that getting our hearts right with Him and others is more important than outward religious displays. We must leave our gifts of worship, "At the altar" and, "First be reconciled." If we do not deal with the sins of our hearts, Satan will spoil our inner peace. "Agree with your adversary quickly," before Satan torments you with demonic bitterness, by unforgiveness. 'Lest Satan should take advantage of us; for we are not ignorant of his devices' (2 Corinthians 2:11).

Day 58

Sin Begins Within

"You have heard that it was said to those of old, 'You shall not commit adultery.' But I say to you that whoever looks at a woman to lust for her has already committed adultery with her in his heart" (Matthew 5:27-28).

Religion often dwells on the outward behaviour of people – if only 'they' will keep rule number one, to rule three hundred they may have a hope of salvation! Contrary to this, Jesus' teaching rejects all the works-based religious systems which focus on the outward appearance, devoid of the heart (1 Thessalonians 2:4). Jesus said, "Woe to you Pharisees! For you tithe mint and rue and all manner of herbs, and pass by justice and the love of God. These you ought to have done, without leaving the others undone" (Luke 11:42-43).

Christ educates us that it is not our outward appearance of religion which counts, but the test of our hearts before God. He not only sees the practical manifestation of our sins, but also the inward birthing of sin. We are warned to deal with the inner secret battles of the heart, which will help lead us to holiness. Sexual sin does not begin when a certain set of bad circumstances prevails, but previously, when the heart has opened itself up to lust. Christ fleshes out the real problem is forever in the heart – just to look at a person and lust, is to commit adultery of the heart (Mark 7:23).

Christianity as a faith does not advocate judging others and focusing on their sins or failings, rather Christ encourages all to look inward. We are to judge, test and weigh our own hearts (2 Corinthians 13:5). We are not called to appear to have kept a certain set of rules out of religious duty, but to make our hearts right before God, leading to holy actions.

Paul wrote of the dangers of 'self-imposed' religion. 'If you died with Christ from the basic principles of the world, why, as though living in the world, do you subject yourselves to regulations...according to the commandments and doctrines of men? These things indeed have an appearance of wisdom in self-imposed religion, false humility and neglect of the body, but are of no value against the indulgence of the flesh' (Colossians 2:20-23).

Christ's Yoke is Easy

"You have hidden these things from the wise and prudent and have revealed them to babes...All things have been delivered to Me by My Father and no one knows the Son except the Father. Nor does anyone know the Father except the Son and the one to whom the Son wills to reveal Him. Come to Me, all you who labour and are heavy laden, and I will give you rest. Take My yoke upon you and learn from Me, for I am gentle and lowly in heart, and you will find rest for your souls. For My yoke is easy and My burden is light" (Matthew 11:25-30).

In the Garden of Eden, Adam and Eve were given endless opportunities for joy filled living (Genesis 2:16-17). God, 'Gives us richly all things to enjoy' (1 Timothy 6:17). There was only one thing forbidden – that which led to sin and the knowledge of wickedness fracturing God's perfect world. God never forbade them the good, only the thing which led to evil and it is the same for us. 'Every good gift and every perfect gift is from above, and comes down from the Father of lights, with whom there is no variation' (James 1:17).

Everything God forbids is for our protection. God is good and He cannot make commands which are evil or mean spirited (3 John 11). His yoke of obedience is always lighter than the yoke of sin. When He says, "No," it is because the thing is harmful. This is why He tells us to change direction – to repent – because the road is self-destructive (Titus 3:3).

When we obey God, we find the very things He asked us to give up, were the things which would have killed our spiritual wellbeing, godly relationships and Christian lives. He commands us to repent of all the things which will eventually make us miserable (1 Peter 4:3-6). When we light a match of sin, thinking it is under control, God tells us to put it out, as He sees the small fire getting bigger and consuming all.

Having no peace, joy or right standing with God and being filled with unforgiveness, bitterness, misery, addictions – having hangovers, being controlled by substances and all secret sins is the heavy yoke, which Christ wants to deliver us from. By comparison to the cost of sin, His yoke is light.

Day 60

Death and Resurrection

"If anyone desires to come after Me, let him deny himself, and take up his cross daily and follow Me. For whoever desires to save his life will lose it, but whoever loses his life for My sake will save it" (Luke 9:23-25).

When we were born again our spirits were made new creations (Galatians 6:15); yet our souls (our minds, wills and emotions), still remained worldly (1 John 4:5, 5:19). We are told, 'To be carnally minded is death, but to be spiritually minded is life and peace' (Romans 8:6). In consequence, we must choose to live out of our born again spirit and its desires, rather than from the soulish realm. Deep down in our born again spirit we do not want sin; rather God's will. To do this, we must embrace a process called, 'Death to self.' This takes place when we deny sinful desires, leading to their starvation and death (Galatians 6:14), and embrace Christ's resurrection life (Romans 6:6-12, Philippians 3:10).

Jesus said, "Most assuredly, I say to you, unless a grain of wheat falls into the ground and dies, it remains alone; but if it dies, it produces much grain. He who loves his life will lose it and he who hates his life in this world will keep it for eternal life. If anyone serves Me, let him follow Me; and where I am, there My servant will be also" (John 12:24-25).

We must reject any preaching which nourishes our worldly desires into bloom, as it appeals only to our temporal selfish wants. If our 'faith' focuses on getting God to bless us, to give us more now and is self-centred, it is not Christ's faith (Matthew 6:19, 1 Timothy 4:1). Peter warned of false 'Bible' teachers. 'By covetousness they will exploit you' (2 Peter 2:3). Whenever Christianity is taught to be selfish in nature, it becomes empty, powerless and futile (Luke 11:34).

When Christ evaluated the early churches, He praised those with sacrificial faith, and warned those who thought they were rich and had no needs (Revelation 2:8-11, 3:14-22). What every person needs is not more things, or larger bank accounts, but to be transformed by God (Matthew 6:19-20). Before Christ's resurrection life can transform us, we must first die in Him to this world (Galatians 6:14).

Day 61

God Wants You

"Many will say to Me in that day, 'Lord, Lord, have we not prophesied in Your name, cast out demons in Your name, and done many wonders in Your name?' And then I will declare to them, 'I never knew you; depart from Me, you who practice lawlessness!' " (Matthew 7:22-23).

Knowing God personally, through Christ, by the Holy Spirit is the essential foundation for Christian living (Ephesians 2:18). Jesus explained that He is not looking for our service only, but for us. He does not want our work, He wants our complete devotion – all we are and have (Hebrews 2:13).

We are also told our faith in Christ will be demonstrated by our behaviour, not just by our declarations (James 1:26, 2:20). Christ warns on Judgment Day many will stand before Him thinking they are Christians because they have prophesied in His name, cast out demons in His name and performed many wonders in His name! These people will know the Bible and believe they are saved, and yet they will be denounced. They, "Practice lawlessness." These are people who confess faith in Jesus, whilst still loving sin, without remorse, repentance and have no desire to be holy (1 John 1:9). They may appear to do good works for Christ; nevertheless, the Lord will say to them, "I never knew you."

What does Christ want from us? Jesus said, "You shall love the Lord your God with all your heart, with all your soul and with all your mind. This is the first and great commandment. And the second is like it: You shall love your neighbour as yourself" (Matthew 22:37-39).

God's primary will for our lives is for us to love Him with everything we are and everything we have. He wants us and He desires us to want Him. He loves for us to spend our lives becoming more and more His (2 Thessalonians 1:12), and by doing so, His grace will flow from us to others.

The Bible states: 'A man's heart reveals the man' (Proverbs 27:19). What is in our hearts? Do we love God with everything, or at least, do we desire to love God with all? God does not want good works, He wants pure hearts.

Day 62

Hearing and Applying

"But why do you call Me, 'Lord, Lord,' and not do the things which I say? Whoever comes to Me, and hears My sayings and does them, I will show you whom he is like: He is like a man building a house, who dug deep and laid the foundation on the rock. And when the flood arose, the stream beat vehemently against that house and could not shake it, for it was founded on the rock. But he who heard and did nothing is like a man who built a house on the earth without a foundation, against which the stream beat vehemently; and immediately it fell. And the ruin of that house was great" (Luke 6:46-49).

It is apparent Jesus Christ was particularly concerned by people who say He is their Lord whilst refusing to listen to or apply anything He says! How strange it must be for God to hear people singing songs of adoration and praise of Jesus, whilst choosing to remain ignorant of all He ever said or did! To illustrate His point, the Lord spoke of two homes, one built on the rock of Christ with deep foundations and another on the ever-changing sands of our own opinions, ideas and the world's values. Christ stated that storms will come – the trials of life and the end time storms of judgment, and only those who follow Christ and His teaching will be safe.

We are told that hearing and doing what Christ commands is likened to being, "A wise man," meanwhile, those who hear Jesus' teaching and do not apply it are like, "A foolish man." Are we wise or foolish? The answer is found in how we listen to and apply, or ignore the teaching of Jesus.

Christ said, "Not everyone who says to Me, 'Lord, Lord,' shall enter the Kingdom of Heaven, but he who does the will of My Father in heaven. Many will say to Me in that day, 'Lord, Lord, have we not'…(done all this)…'in Your name?' And then I will declare to them, 'I never knew you; depart from Me, you who practice lawlessness!' " (Matthew 7:21-23). Thus, knowing Christ personally and obeying His Word is key. Our salvation is free, but our obedience is the fruit of our redemption (Ephesians 2:8-10, James 2:20). Do we know Him, or do we practice lawlessness without regard?

Day 63

Jesus and Women

'Many women who followed Jesus from Galilee, ministering to Him, were there looking on from afar, among whom were Mary Magdalene, Mary the mother of James and Joses, and the mother of Zebedee's sons' (Matthew 27:55-56).

Jesus' esteem for women was in stark contrast to the prevailing attitudes of the first century. Christ honoured women with dignity and championed new rights for them (Mark 10:4-9). Christ was also humble enough to receive financial support from 'the overlooked' women (Luke 8:1-3).

The Bible demonstrates that God created both sexes in His image, and imparted to both, separate and wonderful graces to be expressed in them (Genesis 1:26). The Divine nature is conveyed in meaningful ways through the sexes and their union delivers a fuller reflection of God (Ephesians 5:30-33).

Adam defined the world around him, giving it structure and order (Genesis 2:19), whilst Eve walked with God and heard His voice along with Adam. She was entrusted to be the guardian of conception, the protector of the defenceless and the incubator of God's handiwork (Job 10:8-12, Psalm 139:13-16). She birthed life into this world and was tasked with moulding future generations in a spirit of compassion, mercy and grace, to counteract the warrior spirit of Adam (Genesis 3:20, 4:1-14). They were two parts of one design.

Eve's name literally means 'Life,' stressing that women can release life in a variety of roles. Adam could build a house, while Eve made a home (Genesis 2:18). He sought profits, whilst she desired virtuous dealings (Proverbs 31:18, 24).

Jesus denounced the flaws of their laws towards women (Matthew 5:31-32), He showed compassion (Mark 5:31-34), speaking up for their rights – highlighting double standards (John 8:1-11); He ignored segregated culture (John 4:4-42), and wept publicly with Mary and Martha (John 11:35-36).

In God's original plan, women were always going to be co-heirs together in the grace of life (1 Peter 3:7), and destined to be one in Christ. 'There is neither Jew nor Greek, there is neither slave nor free, there is neither male nor female; for you are all one in Christ Jesus' (Galatians 3:28-29).

Day 64

Redemption

'Now He was teaching in one of the synagogues on the Sabbath. And behold, there was a woman who had a spirit of infirmity eighteen years, and was bent over and could in no way raise herself up. But when Jesus saw her, He called her to Him and said to her, "Woman, you are loosed from your infirmity." And He laid His hands on her, and immediately she was made straight and glorified God. But the ruler of the synagogue answered with indignation, because Jesus had healed on the Sabbath; and he said to the crowd, "There are six days on which men ought to work; therefore come and be healed on them, and not on the Sabbath day." The Lord then answered him and said, "Hypocrite! Does not each one of you on the Sabbath loose his ox or donkey from the stall and lead it away to water it? So ought not this woman, being a daughter of Abraham, whom Satan has bound – think of it – for eighteen years, be loosed from this bond on the Sabbath?" And when He said these things, all His adversaries were put to shame; and all the multitude rejoiced for all the glorious things that were done by Him' (Luke 13:10-17).

The role of women in Bible days was vastly different from what we now experience. The closest we can get to glimpse what the life of first century woman was, is the oppressive regime in Saudi Arabia, where women are treated as second class citizens. Jesus disregarded all the oppression and religious hypocrisy of His age to champion women, who also needed God's mercy. In the case of this healing, Christ explained that this woman was also an heir of Abraham, who was bound by Satan. How could you help an animal, but not a person? How sad religion without Christ can be!

Tax collectors – the collaborators with Rome and harlots were at the bottom of Jewish society, but Jesus taught both could be redeemed (Matthew 21:32). He proved men and women should bare equal responsibility for their sin and both can be forgiven (John 8:1-11). In His darkest hours, the men ran from Jesus, whilst the women stayed, helped bury Him and met the risen Christ (Mark 15:47, John 19:25).

Day 65

The Marriage Covenant

"From the beginning of the creation, God made them male and female. 'For this reason a man shall leave his father and mother and be joined to his wife, and the two shall become one flesh;' so then they are no longer two, but one flesh" (Mark 10:6-8).

When a man and a woman are married, the two become one in God's sight and this union paints a veiled reflection of Christ's oneness with His Church (Ephesians 5:30-33). By the standards of modern Western culture, marriage is simply two individuals making an emotional promise to each other, which may not last (Proverbs 20:25). Our culture changes, but not Christ's standards. He tells us marriage is the joining of one male and female for life, in a sacred covenant before God. The marriage covenant is a spiritually watertight agreement sealed by God (Matthew 19:4-6), that cannot be broken consequence free (Numbers 30:2, Malachi 2:14-15).

God does not accept the cheapening or devaluing of the marriage covenant (Ecclesiastes 5:2-7, Jeremiah 31:32-33, Ephesians 5:30-33). God does not consent to the tearing up of any covenant, because our salvation depends on Him keeping His covenant with us (Matthew 26:28). God exhibits sacrificial faithfulness and enduring love to us, and He urges all to do the same (Jeremiah 3:1, Luke 6:32, John 15:13).

For these reasons Christians can never enter into marriage lightly, never with an unbeliever (2 Corinthians 6:14-16), and it cannot be exited with ease. To God, covenant is always greater than the individual because it regards one's vow before Him of provision to another, and the safety and wellbeing of any children birthed within the marriage. In such cases, the marriage covenant is a guarantee that the two individuals will put self to one side, in the best interests of any offspring. This is what Christ did by coming to earth – He put self interest on the altar, so we could be united with the Father, as His children (Hebrews 2:13). Christ made a covenant at great cost, to benefit us for eternity. As a result, covenant is the exact opposite of selfishness; it is selfless and sacrificially steadfast (Hosea 6:6-7).

Day 66

Marriage is Sacred

'The Pharisees asked, "Is it lawful for a man to divorce his wife *for just any reason?*" And He answered and said to them, "Have you not read that He who made them at the beginning made them male and female, and said, 'For this reason a man shall leave his father and mother and be joined to his wife, and the two shall become one flesh?' So then, they are no longer two but one flesh. Therefore what God has joined together, let not man separate." They said to Him, "Why then did Moses command to give a certificate of divorce and to put her away?" He said to them, "Moses, because of the hardness of your hearts, permitted you to divorce your wives, but from the beginning it was not so. And I say to you, whoever divorces his wife, except for sexual immorality and marries another, commits adultery; and whoever marries her who is divorced commits adultery" (Matthew 19:3-9).

In these verses we are given an insight into the treatment of women in Jesus' day and how His teaching could improve their rights. Men could search for 'any reason' to divorce their wives and to give them a certificate of divorce, as they abandoned their responsibilities and covenant before God. Women without an income would have been in terrible trouble; but Jesus establishes from the beginning the value of all covenant marriage relationships. This teaching was not designed to condemn divorcees, but to rejuvenate marriage.

The prophet Malachi warns God despises fervent religious emotional displays, when the marriage covenant is ignored. "You cover the altar of the Lord with tears, with weeping and crying. So He does not regard the offering anymore, nor receive it with goodwill from your hands. Yet you say, 'For what reason?' Because the Lord has been witness between you and the wife of your youth, with whom you have dealt treacherously. Yet she is your companion and your wife by covenant. But did He not make them one, having a remnant of the Spirit? And why one? He seeks godly offspring. 'Therefore take heed to your spirit and let none deal treacherously with the wife of his youth' " (Malachi 2:13-15).

Day 67

Marriage or Singleness

Jesus' disciples said, "If such is the case of the man with his wife, it is better not to marry." But He said, "All cannot accept this, but only those to whom it has been given: For there are eunuchs who were born thus from their mother's womb and there are eunuchs who were made eunuchs by men, and there are eunuchs who have made themselves eunuchs for the Kingdom of Heaven's sake. He who is able to accept it, let him accept it" (Matthew 19:10-12).

Christ has something to say to believers about every area of their lives and His plan is complete in its fullness. Jesus offers His disciples two choices for their lives – either to be single and celibate, or married for life and faithful (Matthew 19:11-12). When the Lord stated His strict rules concerning the binding matter of the marriage covenant, His disciples were shocked. They argued it would be better to remain single, than to be bound in a watertight marriage covenant.

Jesus permitted divorce in cases of "sexual immorality" (Matthew 5:32), and Paul espouses freedom if abandoned (1 Corinthians 7:15). However, followers of Jesus are called to live to high standards, because God has revealed His will in the matters of sex, marriage and the value of covenant.

Sexual immorality, adultery and promiscuity are a great offence to God. 'Marriage is honourable among all and the bed undefiled; but fornicators (those who have sex outside of marriage), and adulterers God will judge' (Hebrews 13:4).

Many have asked, "What is God's will for me?" The Word of God reveals His written will, as we await His personal will. 'For this is the will of God, your sanctification: that you should abstain from sexual immorality; that each of you should know how to possess his own vessel in sanctification and honour, not in passion of lust, like the Gentiles who do not know God; that no one should take advantage of and defraud his brother in this matter, because the Lord is the avenger of all such, as we also forewarned you and testified. For God did not call us to uncleanness, but in holiness. Therefore he who rejects this does not reject man, but God, who has given us His Holy Spirit' (1 Thessalonians 4:3-8).

Day 68

Suffering

'There were present at that season some who told Him about the Galileans whose blood Pilate had mingled with their sacrifices. And Jesus answered and said to them, "Do you suppose that these Galileans were worse sinners than all other Galileans, because they suffered such things? I tell you, no; but unless you repent you will all likewise perish. Or those eighteen on whom the tower in Siloam fell and killed them, do you think that they were worse sinners than all other men who dwelt in Jerusalem? I tell you, no; but unless you repent you will all likewise perish" (Luke 13:1-5).

In history, diverse generations have focused on parts of the Bible to the detriment of their biblical counterbalance. Today many preachers proclaim the, "Everything will be great," message to gain hearers. Of course, in the end everything will be great, but this was not the full message of Jesus.

Throughout the Middle Ages, Christians in general did not believe they would be happy, blessed and prosperous, etc. They suffered much in life and were reminded that Adam's fall led to suffering being a part of life, and all would never be perfect until Christ's return. Life would be hard, death had entered and, "In the sweat of your face you shall eat bread, till you return to the ground. For out of it you were taken. For dust you are and to dust you shall return" (Genesis 3:19).

Those Christians may have focused too much on suffering and not enough on the promises of God's aid, yet perhaps we focus too much on the good, to the detriment of biblical reality (John 15:18-21). When Jesus spoke of the Galileans' blood and the victims of the Siloam tower disaster, He told His followers that bad things happen to people who are no guiltier than others. He urged all to repent because it is only in heaven when all the wrongs of earth will be put right.

Unfortunately, suffering is part of life; yet God does redeem goodness from hardship (2 Peter 1:5-9). When all is well, we tend to focus on the pleasures of now; but when in trouble, we often seek the Lord and focus our hearts on eternity, to our true benefit. 'Sorrow is better than laughter, for by a sad countenance the heart is made better' (Ecclesiastes 7:3).

Day 69

The Suffering Saviour

"Ought not the Christ to suffer these things?" (Luke 24:26).

Christ never promised to save us from suffering; instead He has walked before us and drunk the cup of suffering to the full. He made a choice to embrace infliction as a human and as such, is able to sympathise with all we experience (Hebrews 4:15). When we suffer, Christ does not say to us, "See you on the other side," but He comforts us by the Holy Spirit. 'God is...a very present help in trouble' (Psalm 46:1, James 5:10, 1 Peter 2:21). We may not 'feel' Him, yet we recall He has already walked these steps far ahead of us, and His footprints were far deeper than ours will ever be.

The burden of the sin and suffering of the entire world came upon Christ in His Passion, and He overcame in order to give us the opportunity to rise with Him in His resurrection (Philippians 3:10). Just as we die with Him and share in His sufferings, we will also be raised in Him (Philippians 3:10).

Christ does not stand at a distance from all who suffer; He has already shared in the horrors of this world. His parents feared a pregnancy scandal (Matthew 1:19), He was born very poor (Luke 2:24), and His family had to flee their nation due to cruel persecution, as He became a refugee in Egypt (Matthew 2:13-18). He returned to Israel and lived under occupation, and suffered the loss of his father, at what must have been a young age; whilst people He knew said He was, "Out of His mind" (Mark 3:21). The religious called Him mad and demonised (John 10:20), and His family and other locals were offended by His ministry (Matthew 13:55). Jesus was impoverished and had no home for many years (Luke 9:58), and He was often provided for by the lowliest of all in His culture (Luke 8:3). The Lord was rejected by His own people, abandoned by His disciples, suffered humiliation, and was condemned in an illegal trial. He was beaten by the authorities, suffered prolonged torture and was murdered by His government (Matthew 26:47-27:50).

When we suffer Christ knows exactly what it means, as His Holy Spirit, the Comforter comes to strengthen us when we are weak, to help us endure (John 16:7, James 5:11).

Day 70

Divine Healing

'A centurion came to Him, pleading with Him, saying, "Lord, my servant is lying at home paralyzed, dreadfully tormented." And Jesus said to him, "I will come and heal him." The centurion answered and said, "Lord, I am not worthy that You should come under my roof. But only speak a Word and my servant will be healed... When Jesus heard it, He marvelled and said to those who followed, "Assuredly, I say to you, I have not found such great faith, not even in Israel! And I say to you that many will come from east and west, and sit down with Abraham, Isaac, and Jacob in the Kingdom of Heaven"... Jesus said to the centurion, "Go your way; and as you have believed, so let it be done for you." His servant was healed that same hour' (Matthew 8:5-13).

One of the key features of Jesus' ministry was miraculous healing and because, 'Jesus Christ is the same yesterday, today and forever' (Hebrews 13:8), we can still believe for healings. James encouraged the sick to, 'Call for the elders of the church and let them pray over him, anointing him with oil in the name of the Lord. And the prayer of faith will save the sick, and the Lord will raise him up' (James 5:14-15).

Jesus warned that unbelief is a hinderance to witnessing miracles and healings (Matthew 13:58), and He explained we may witness one person being healed, whilst others are still in need (Luke 4:27). Paul was sick (2 Corinthians 12:5-10), and Timothy's frequent illnesses led to practical aid (1 Timothy 5:23); Paul also had to leave Trophimus because he was ill (2 Timothy 4:20). These men had seen the Holy Spirit's gifts of healings and miracles at work, nevertheless they still had physical problems, as they accepted they were still living in the unredeemed body of death (Romans 7:24).

Healings can and do take place today, and in the Bible we find that signs, wonders and healings, as in the case of the centurion, are often given to help people find faith in Christ. Jesus said, "Many," from all over the world will sit down with Him in His Kingdom. If the temporal healing of a body which will still die (1 Corinthians 15:52-54), helps to save a soul, then the manifestation of power has proved its eternal worth.

Day 71

The Outward Man is Still Perishing

'When He came near the gate of the city, behold, a dead man was being carried out, the only son of his mother; and she was a widow...He had compassion on her and said to her, "Do not weep." Then He came and touched the open coffin...And He said, "Young man, I say to you, arise." So he who was dead sat up and began to speak....They glorified God, saying..."God has visited His people" ' (Luke 7:11-16).

When you were born again it was your spirit which came alive. Jesus said, "That which is born of the flesh is flesh and that which is born of the Spirit is spirit. Do not marvel that I said to you, 'You must be born again' " (John 3:6-8).

Deep in our spirit we were made new creations in Christ (2 Corinthians 5:17), and the seed of His resurrection life was sown into our spirits (1 John 3:9). Now, it is our job to water this seed to grow and consume our souls. We do this by surrendering our lives to the Holy Spirit, as we also seek to renew our minds to think on God's will (Romans 12:1-2).

Christ died for our full redemption – spirit, soul and body. The redemption of our spirits took place immediately after conversion, as we were, 'Sealed with the Holy Spirit of promise' (Ephesians 1:13). Now, the renewing of our souls is subject to our obedience to live holy and renew our minds (Colossians 3:10), with the hope of full transformation (1 Corinthians 15:49). But our bodies are still natural, subject to death, awaiting their redemption (1 Corinthians 15:50-54). In other words, we still reside in the 'body of death' (Romans 7:24). When we were born again, our physical bodies did not change miraculously – they will die like everyone's, unless Christ comes. The Bible states: 'Elisha had become sick with the illness of which he would die' (2 Kings 13:14), and Paul wrote: 'Even though our outward man is perishing, yet the inward man is being renewed day by day' (2 Corinthians 4:16). Christ died for the full redemption of our bodies and we may witness the grace and gifts of healing – 'By whose stripes you were healed' (1 Peter 2:24). Yet, our bodies continue to get older, which is a sign of the process of death at work, until Christ comes or we go to Him.

Day 72

Death Defeated

'When Mary came where Jesus was and saw Him, she fell down at His feet, saying to Him, "Lord, if You had been here, my brother would not have died." Therefore, when Jesus saw her weeping and the Jews who came with her weeping, He groaned in the spirit, and was troubled. And He said, "Where have you laid him?" They said to Him, "Lord, come and see." Jesus wept' (John 11:32-35).

The shortest verse in the Bible highlights Christ's mourning at a friend's death. In Western culture, we tend to bottle up and subdue grief, whilst in Bible days they had periods to mourn and were encouraged to, 'Let it out' (Genesis 23:2). But there is more. When an astronaut goes into space, he or she puts on a spacesuit which is designed to sustain life in a hostile environment. From a biblical perspective, our bodies are like spacesuits, which one day must be 'put off,' so we can enter into the presence of Jesus. Peter described his earthly body as a tent. 'Shortly I must put off my tent, just as our Lord Jesus Christ showed me' (2 Peter 1:14).

For Christians, death is something uniquely different from the world's paradigm. Death was once our enemy (Romans 5:17), as it announced the end of life (1 Corinthians 15:26). Yet, Christ broke this enemy and forced it to comply with His will (Revelation 1:18). In Christ's hands the great enemy has become His means of liberation! He uses death to liberate our souls and spirits from our earthly bodies, to bring us home to God (Romans 7:24-25). 'For our citizenship is in heaven, from which we also eagerly wait for the Saviour, the Lord Jesus Christ, who will transform our lowly body that it may be conformed to His glorious body' (Philippians 3:20-21). Thus, we follow Christ in death and come out the other side in the, 'Likeness of His resurrection' (Romans 6:5).

Heaven is real and in God's home we will never need to battle with sin, sickness, bad thoughts or struggle with the carnal nature, etc. We will be liberated from all the effects of the fall and will be like little mirrors of Christ.

Thus, we mourn in death, but we know it has lost its sting; this mortal shall put on immortality (1 Corinthians 15:53-55).

Day 73

Playing Games

"Do not lay up for yourselves treasures on earth, where moth and rust destroy, and where thieves break in and steal; but lay up for yourselves treasures in heaven, where neither moth nor rust destroys, and where thieves do not break in and steal" (Matthew 6:19-21).

Monopoly is a board game in which players try to gain dominance on fictional real estate, as pieces advance around the board, according to the throw of dices. When we play this game, it's amazing how serious it can be taken, as players struggle to achieve temporal gain.

On earth, we are playing a form of temporal Monopoly, as eternal reality stalks us. We all seek to find our place on the board of life, earn our living and keep up with others, etc. But when we die, we will look back from eternity and laugh or mourn, at the silly games we played. From heaven or hell, it will appear as if all we had was Monopoly money, homes, businesses, etc. One day the 'board game' of this life will be folded up and we will look eternal reality in the face. If we used our gifts and talents to store up earthly treasure, it will all turn out to be like Monopoly money. But if we put Christ and His Kingdom first, all of our money, time, energy and effort will be converted into eternal crowns, rewards and blessings which never fade (Matthew 16:27, Mark 9:41).

Christians are commanded to provide for those they are responsible for (1 Timothy 5:8), and we are encouraged to prepare and save for the future (Proverbs 13:22). But Jesus is also clear that our treasures are not to be found or sought after in this life; we are citizens of heaven (Philippians 3:20).

If we take Jesus' Kingdom teaching seriously, we will be concerned to know there are billions of people who have never truly heard the gospel and there are millions of poor Christians who cannot afford a Bible. Therefore, how can we declare we love Jesus (1 John 3:17), whilst ignoring His command to make disciples of all nations? Jesus said, "If you love Me, keep My commandments" (John 14:15). Consequently, our love for God is demonstrated by all we do, not by what we sing, say in prayer, or testify in church.

Day 74

Who Do You Serve?

"No servant can serve two masters; for either he will hate the one and love the other, or else he will be loyal to the one and despise the other. You cannot serve God and mammon" (Luke 16:13).

Jesus stipulates we must put Him first in every area of our lives, especially in the domain of finances. Either Christ's will is first in our decision making or mammon is first. What are our priorities? What are we living for, Christ or more things?

The Christian who puts Christ first in every area of his or her life may not have the quantity of products which non-believers have, but he or she will have the quality of peace which others seek. We may never own mansions, several cars, or holiday abroad twice a year, but all these things are a means to an end. We chase wealth, success, career advancement, relationships, titles and positions of influence in our churches because we think 'they' will provide us with what we truly need – satisfaction, contentment, peace and joy. Christ tells us not to seek what non-believers lust after, but to put God and His Kingdom first (Matthew 6:32-33).

Since the 1960s, the West has experienced growth in personal and expendable incomes, but all surveys reveal we are less content than our poorer forefathers. We have been unhappy as consumers, whilst many of them learnt to be content with the little they had (Philippians 4:12). Many today have been servants of money, to great cost. 'For the love of money is a root of all kinds of evil, for which some have strayed from the faith in their greediness and pierced themselves through with many sorrows' (1 Timothy 6:10).

Christ urges us to accept that life on earth is not all there is. In this life, the goal of believers is not to seek self-worth by what we own or earn, but to live 'in Christ.' It is in the next life where we will be greatly rewarded for all the sacrifices we made for Him. In heaven, there are no more needy souls to serve, no more sacrifices to make, no more unreached people who need a missionary and no more poor Christians who need Bibles. If we are to do anything which will echo in eternity, we must do it now, or never!

Day 75

True Treasure

"For where your treasure is, there your heart will be also" (Luke 12:34).

What we love, we sacrifice for. What we choose to spend our time doing, expend our money on and focus our minds on, is what we love. This is our treasure. Christ does not find what we value by what we sing, proclaim or what we do to be seen, but by what is in our hearts (1 Thessalonians 2:4).

One of the reasons Christ asks us to sacrifice things we enjoy in this life, is to prove to ourselves and to Him, that we really love God first and foremost. It is very easy to sing, "I love you Lord," without it costing us anything; Jesus' instruction brings to the fore that our actions speak louder than our words. What is our treasure?

If we spend our lives seeking to outdo others, this desire will overcome us and our love for the Lord (1 John 2:15). We have not been put on earth to consume and aim to be the best. 'For the love of money is a root of all kinds of evil' (1 Timothy 6:10). The source of this evil is not money, which can be used for good in the Kingdom of God or evil in the world, but the love of money in and of itself. We could ask: What do we spend our time on? What do we do with our money? How much time do we spend thinking about the Lord's will, compared to our desires? Are we striving to be better than others, or to help others find God?

Paul confirms that everything we do in this life will one day be tested by the fire of God's judgment (1 Corinthians 3:11-15). If all we achieve manifests itself out of love of money and pride, we need to repent. If we do good works for selfish motives, we will lose any reward. However, all we do in obedience to God with a pure heart will be rewarded!

This life is not the time for us to sit back, rest and store up riches and to make 'a name' for ourselves. We all need money, rest and balance in our lives, yet it is now or never for us (Romans 13:11). We can make a full surrender to the values of this world, and chase our tails seeking popularity, wealth and prestige or we can give back to God the gifts and talents He gave us, and let Him use them as He will.

Day 76

God the Holy Spirit

'On the last day, that great day of the feast, Jesus stood and cried out, saying, "If anyone thirsts, let him come to Me and drink. He who believes in Me, as the Scripture has said, out of his heart will flow rivers of living water." But this He spoke concerning the Spirit, whom those believing in Him would receive; for the Holy Spirit was not yet given, because Jesus was not yet glorified' (John 7:37-39).

The outpouring of the Holy Spirit is central to the ongoing ministry of God on earth (John 16:7-15). The Bible explains God is revealed as three Persons in One (Matthew 28:19, 2 Corinthians 13:14). 'God (the Father) anointed Jesus of Nazareth (the Son) with the Holy Spirit and with power' (Acts 10:38). Peter said, "Ananias, why has Satan filled your heart to lie to the Holy Spirit?...you have not lied to men but to God" (Acts 5:3-4). It was the Father who sent the Son and the Son sent the Spirit (John 3:16, 16:7). To get to know the Father we need to go through the Door of the Son, and the Spirit seals and regenerates us (John 3:3, 7, 14:7, 2 Timothy 2:19). The Holy Spirit bears witness we are God's children (John 1:12, 15:26), and if we want to receive the Father and the Son, we must also receive the Holy Spirit's indwelling (Matthew 11:27, Luke 10:22, John 5:19-26, 8:28, 14:13).

The Holy Spirit was sent to glorify Jesus. "But when the Helper comes, whom I shall send to you from the Father, the Spirit of Truth who proceeds from the Father, He will testify of Me. And you also will bear witness, because you have been with Me from the beginning" (John 15:26-27).

The manifestations of the ministry of the Holy Spirit in our lives were clarified by Jesus in the Great Commission. 'He said to them, "Go into all the world and preach the gospel to every creature. He who believes and is baptized will be saved; but he who does not believe will be condemned. And these signs will follow those who believe: In My name they will cast out demons; they will speak with new tongues; they will take up serpents; and if they drink anything deadly, it will by no means hurt them; they will lay hands on the sick and they will recover" (Mark 16:15-18).

Day 77

We All Need the Holy Spirit

"If anyone loves Me, he will keep My Word and My Father will love him, and We will come to him and make Our home with him. He who does not love Me does not keep My Words; and the Word which you hear is not Mine but the Father's who sent Me. These things I have spoken to you while being present with you. But the Helper, the Holy Spirit, whom the Father will send in My name, He will teach you all things and bring to your remembrance all things that I said to you. Peace I leave with you, My peace I give to you; not as the world gives do I give to you. Let not your heart be troubled, neither let it be afraid. You have heard Me say to you, 'I am going away and coming back to you.' If you loved Me, you would rejoice because I said, 'I am going to the Father,' for My Father is greater than I. And now I have told you before it comes, that when it does come to pass, you may believe" (John 14:23-29).

Many times Jesus told His disciples of His coming death, resurrection and ascension. As they did not fully understand the prophecies in Scripture, many thought Christ was setting up an earthly temporal Kingdom in Israel, in their day. After His resurrection they still asked, "Lord, will You at this time restore the kingdom to Israel?" And He said to them, "It is not for you to know times or seasons which the Father has put in His own authority. But you shall receive power when the Holy Spirit has come upon you; and you shall be witnesses to Me in Jerusalem, and in all Judea and Samaria, and to the end of the earth" (Acts 1:6-8).

Before His ascension, Jesus stated the Holy Spirit would come to continue His ministry on earth (John 16:7-15). The Holy Spirit is the Helper, "Whom the Father will send in My name." Jesus told us the Spirit would teach us and bring His teaching to our remembrance. He told His disciples to wait for the Holy Spirit, before they went out to make disciples of all nations, because they needed to receive the indwelling Spirit of God. They had received the seal of the Spirit at their conversion (John 20:22, Ephesians 1:13, 4:30); now they needed to be immersed in God (Acts 2:1-47) – as do we!

Day 78

Our Advantage

"It is to your advantage that I go away; for if I do not go away, the Helper will not come to you; but if I depart, I will send Him to you. And when He has come, He will convict the world of sin and of righteousness, and of judgment: of sin, because they do not believe in Me; of righteousness, because I go to My Father and you see Me no more; of judgment, because the ruler of this world is judged. I still have many things to say to you, but you cannot bear them now. However, when He, the Spirit of Truth has come, He will guide you into all truth; for He will not speak on His own authority, but whatever He hears He will speak; and He will tell you things to come. He will glorify Me, for He will take of what is Mine and declare it to you. All things that the Father has are Mine. Therefore I said that He will take of Mine and declare it to you. A little while and you will not see Me; and again a little while and you will see Me, because I go to the Father" (John 16:7-15).

As Christ's ministry led towards the penultimate events of His death, resurrection and ascension into heaven, He told His disciples, "It is to your advantage that I go away," in order for the Helper, the Holy Spirit, God on earth to come. First the Spirit of God comes to convict us of our sin, then, "He will guide you into all truth," to glorify Jesus. The Spirit's ministry in our lives is to be tremendous! "Whatever He hears He will speak and He will tell you things to come."

In the book of Acts, we have the chronicles of how God the Holy Spirit spoke and led the disciples of Jesus. 'As they ministered to the Lord and fasted, the Holy Spirit said, "Now separate to Me Barnabas and Saul for the work to which I have called them"...So, being sent out by the Holy Spirit, they went..."For it seemed good to the Holy Spirit and to us, to lay upon you no greater burden than these necessary things"...They were forbidden by the Holy Spirit to preach the Word in Asia...they tried to go into Bithynia, but the Spirit did not permit them' (Acts 13:2, 4, 15:28, 16:6-7).

You can learn more about the ministry, Person and power of the Holy Spirit in my book *Holy Spirit Power*.

Day 79

Ask for the Holy Spirit

"Whoever drinks the water I give them will never thirst. Indeed, the water I give them will become in them a spring of water welling up to eternal life" (John 4:14).

The indwelling of the Holy Spirit is distinct and separate from our conversion experience. Jesus' disciples were born again and they received the seal of the Spirit when Jesus breathed on them saying, "Receive the Holy Spirit" (John 20:22). We too may have confessed faith in Christ and been sealed by the Spirit (Ephesians 1:13, 4:30), nevertheless, just like the disciples we must wait, "For the promise of My Father" (Luke 24:49). Jesus said, "But you shall be baptised with the Holy Spirit not many days from now" (Acts 1:4-5).

The disciples obeyed the Lord by waiting and, 'When the Day of Pentecost had fully come, they were all with one accord in one place. And suddenly there came a sound from heaven, as of a rushing mighty wind, and it filled the whole house where they were sitting. Then there appeared to them divided tongues, as of fire, and one sat upon each of them. And they were all filled with the Holy Spirit and began to speak with other tongues, as the Spirit gave them utterance' (Acts 2:1-4). After this, the disciples were urgent that every believer in Jesus should receive the indwelling of the Holy Spirit, as Christ commanded. 'They sent Peter and John to them, who, when they had come down, prayed for them that they might receive the Holy Spirit...then they laid hands on them and they received the Holy Spirit' (Acts 8:14-17).

Paul had a similar experience of being born again first and later being indwelt by the Holy Spirit. Paul was saved and sealed (Acts 9:1-6), and then three days later received the baptism of the Holy Spirit (Acts 9:9, 17). Paul later learnt to become sensitive to the voice and leading of the Holy Spirit. 'The Holy Spirit testifies in every city, saying...' and, 'They told Paul through the Spirit...' (Acts 20:23, 21:4).

All Christians must ask the Holy Spirit to come and enter them, to glorify Jesus Christ (1 Corinthians 6:19). The Lord urges us, saying, "How much more will your heavenly Father give the Holy Spirit to those who ask Him!" (Luke 11:13).

Day 80

Who Do Men Say I Am?

'Jesus asked His disciples, saying to them, "Who do men say that I am?" So they answered, "John the Baptist; but some say, Elijah; and others, one of the prophets." He said to them, "But who do you say that I am?" Peter answered and said to Him, "You are the Christ" ' (Mark 8:27-29).

Some have claimed Jesus was only a good teacher, a human prophet and many other things, but who did Jesus say He was and is? What does the Truth Himself state?

Jesus said, "I am the Bread of Life. He who comes to Me shall never hunger and He who believes in Me shall never thirst (John 6:35). I am the Light of the World, he who follows Me shall not walk in darkness, but have the light of life (John 8:12). I am the Door. If anyone enters by Me, He will be saved, and will go in and out and find pasture (John 10:9). I am the Good Shepherd. The Good Shepherd gives His life for the sheep (John 10:11). I am the Resurrection and the Life. He who believes in Me, though he may die, he shall live (John 11:25). I have come that they may have life and that they may have it more abundantly (John 10:10). I am the Way, the Truth and the Life (John 14:6). Whoever drinks of the water that I shall give him will never thirst. But the water that I shall give him will become in him a fountain of water springing up into everlasting life" (John 4:14).

Jesus taught He existed before the foundation of the world (Micah 5:2, John 17:24), and He came from heaven (John 6:41-42). He explained He was alive before Abraham (John 8:58), and He said Moses testified of Him (John 5:39). He stated He was and is equal with God the Father (John 10:30-33, 14:9, 17:5), and by His works He proved His Divinity (John 14:11). Jesus said, "I and My Father are One" (John 10:30), and He expected to be honoured exactly the same as God the Father in heaven (John 5:23). Jesus told people He could forgive sins, as only God can (Luke 7:48), and He freed people from condemnation (John 8:7-11).

Jesus knew who He was and so did His disciples. Today, His question is asked of us -"But who do you say that I am?"

Day 81

Jesus, One with the Father

"I told you and you do not believe. The works that I do in My Father's name, they bear witness of Me. But you do not believe, because you are not of My sheep, as I said to you. My sheep hear My voice and I know them, and they follow Me. And I give them eternal life, and they shall never perish; neither shall anyone snatch them out of My hand. My Father, who has given them to Me, is greater than all; and no one is able to snatch them out of My Father's hand. I and My Father are One" (John 10:25-30).

The Gospel of John chronicles many of the debates and contentions Jesus had with the religious leaders of His day. Due to His miracles they knew He had a legitimate claim to be the Messiah. The Old Testament is filled with prophecies concerning the life and work of the Messiah, and Jesus was fulfilling them! When John the Baptist was discouraged in prison, Christ reminded him of Isaiah's signs of the Messiah (Isaiah 35:5-6). Jesus said, "Go and tell John the things you have seen and heard: that the blind see, the lame walk, the lepers are cleansed, the deaf hear, the dead are raised and the poor have the gospel preached to them" (Luke 7:22-23).

The apostles chronicled who Jesus was and is. They called Him: Immanuel, meaning God with us (Matthew 1:23, 25), Son of God, meaning equal to God (John 1:34, 10:30-33), Messiah (John 1:41), Holy One (Mark 1:24), Saviour (2 Peter 2:20), Son of the Highest (Luke 1:23), Lord of all (Acts 10:36), and Lord God Almighty (Revelation 15:3).

Jesus is the Lamb of God (John 1:29), the Lion of the Tribe of Judah (Revelation 5:5), the Prince of Life (Acts 3:15), the Word of Life (John 1:1), the Light of the World (John 8:12), the Chief Shepherd (1 Peter 5:4), the Advocate (1 John 2:1), the Righteous Judge (2 Timothy 4:8), the Author and Finisher of our Faith (Hebrews 12:2), the Alpha and Omega, the Beginning and the End (Revelation 1:8), and the King of kings and the Lord of lords (Revelation 19:6). He is the same today, yesterday and forevermore (Hebrews 13:8). Finally, the apostles warned many false teachers would deny Christ's Deity (Colossians 2:6-10, 1 John 2:22-23).

Day 82

The Last Supper

"The Son of Man indeed goes just as it is written of Him, but woe to that man by whom the Son of Man is betrayed!"…And as they were eating, Jesus took bread, blessed and broke it, and gave it to them and said, "Take, eat; this is My body." Then He took the cup and when He had given thanks He gave it to them, and they all drank from it. And He said to them, "This is My blood of the new covenant, which is shed for many. Assuredly, I say to you, I will no longer drink of the fruit of the vine until that day when I drink it new in the Kingdom of God" (Mark 14:21-25).

Christ's suffering, His torture, death and rising again to life had all been foretold by the prophets, and Jesus had tried to prepare the disciples for His forthcoming Passion. The Lord was anointed for burial (Mark 14:6-9), but His disciples did not understand. Jesus celebrated the Passover with the full knowledge that one sitting at His table would betray Him (Mark 14:17-22). He instituted the Lord's Supper, teaching all His followers to remember on a regular basis, His broken body and shed blood (1 Corinthians 11:23-26).

The Lord told His disciples, in fulfilment of the prophecy of Scripture, "All of you will be made to stumble because of Me this night, for it is written: 'I will strike the Shepherd and the sheep will be scattered.' But after I have been raised, I will go before you to Galilee" (Mark 14:27-28).

Christ had already foreseen His resurrected life in Galilee (Mark 16:7), but first a terrible crucifixion awaited Him. In the Garden of Gethsemane, He said, "My soul is exceedingly sorrowful, even to death" (Mark 14:34), and He fell to the ground and prayed, "Abba, Father, all things are possible for You. Take this cup away from Me; nevertheless, not what I will, but what You will" (Mark 14:36).

That very night, the Lord was betrayed by Judas and was arrested by officers of the religious leaders, in collusion with the Romans (John 18:3-4). He said, "Have you come out, as against a robber, with swords and clubs to take Me? I was daily with you in the temple teaching and you did not seize Me. But the Scriptures must be fulfilled" (Mark 14:48-49).

Day 83

The Religious Leaders, the Disciples and Jesus

"I put You under oath by the living God: Tell us if You are the Christ, the Son of God!" Jesus said to him, "It is as you said. Nevertheless, I say to you, hereafter you will see the Son of Man sitting at the right hand of the Power and coming on the clouds of heaven." Then the high priest tore his clothes saying, "He has spoken blasphemy! What further need do we have of witnesses? Look, now you have heard His blasphemy!" (Matthew 26:63-65).

The religious leaders in Jesus' day knew that He declared Himself to be God – 'Therefore the Jews sought all the more to kill Him, because He not only broke the Sabbath, but also said that God was His Father, making Himself equal with God' (John 5:18). They said, "Why does this Man speak blasphemies like this? Who can forgive sins but God alone?" (Mark 2:7). Jesus was a grave threat to the broken religious system of His day because He qualified the Law of Moses (Mark 10:4-12), fulfilling the Law (Matthew 5:17-20), and He explained He would ascend into heaven to fulfil all things (John 6:61-62, Acts 1:9, 1 Peter 3:22). Jesus stated by His command the dead will be raised to life (John 5:25), and He maintained His power, as God, to give eternal life (John 17:2); He will be the Judge in the afterlife (Matthew 19:28).

Jesus told His disciples He was going to lay down His life willingly and would rise from the dead (John 10:11-18). He explained He would give everlasting life to all those who believed in Him (John 5:24), and to prove this He exercised His power to bring people back from the dead (John 10:18).

Those who lived with Jesus testified He could heal the sick (Mark 1:34), and raise the deceased (Luke 7:14-15, 8:52, John 11:43). They witnessed Him controlling and multiplying food (John 6:1-14), and as God, He commanded nature (Psalm 107:25-29, Luke 8:22-25, John 6:15-21).

One by one, as heavenly revelation came to the disciples, they worshipped Christ as God (Matthew 14:33, 28:17, John 20:28). Lastly, all of Christ's disciples were prepared to die for their faith in Him, as they testified of His Divinity to others (Luke 24:52), and declared Him to be God in their letters.

Day 84

Christ's Six Trials

'The high priest stood up in the midst and asked Jesus, saying, "Do You answer nothing? What is it these men testify against You?" But He kept silent and answered nothing. Again the high priest asked Him, saying to Him, "Are You the Christ, the Son of the Blessed?" Jesus said, "I am. And you will see the Son of Man sitting at the right hand of the Power and coming with the clouds of heaven." Then the high priest tore his clothes and said, "What further need do we have of witnesses? You have heard the blasphemy! What do you think?" And they all condemned Him to be deserving of death. Then some began to spit on Him and to blindfold Him, and to beat Him, and to say to Him, "Prophesy!" And the officers struck Him with the palms of their hands' (Mark 14:60-65).

In His Passion Jesus endured six trials, one for each day of creation. Two trials were held at night illegally, when all of the religious leaders were unable to attend. During the three initial religious trials, the Lord suffered a preliminary hearing before Annas (John 18:12-24), followed by the formal illegal night questioning before the high priest Caiaphas (Mark 14:53-65). In the morning, the Sanhedrin, as representatives of Israel and all the Jews, publicly rejected their Messiah, as Caiaphas condemned their King (Luke 22:66-71).

Afterwards Jesus was taken for His first hearing before the secular authorities. Initially He went before Pilate (John 18:28-37), who sensed no threat from Jesus Christ and did not believe He was guilty of any crime. Pilate, 'Went out again to the Jews and said to them, "I find no fault in Him at all" ' (John 18:38). The Lord was then sent to be questioned by Herod (Luke 23:6-12), and finally, He was condemned in His final hearing before Pilate, who stated a flogging would suffice. However, the religious leaders stirred up the mob at Jerusalem to reject Christ, calling for His crucifixion and for the release of a thief (Matthew 27:15-26). Jesus said to Pilate, "You could have no power at all against Me unless it had been given you from above. Therefore the one who delivered Me to you has the greater sin" (John 19:11).

Day 85

A Convenient Time

'When Herod saw Jesus, he was exceedingly glad; for he had desired for a long time to see Him, because he had heard many things about Him and he hoped to see some miracle done by Him. Then he questioned Him with many words, but He answered him nothing' (Luke 23:8-10).

In Jesus' second civil trial, He stood before Herod. In the time of Christ, in the Roman province of Judea, there were many whose only concern was for the cares of this life. Jesus said, "But take heed to yourselves, lest your hearts be weighed down with carousing, drunkenness and cares of this life" (Luke 21:34). Countless numbers were fighting hard for their living and were busy talking about who will marry who, what businesses were thriving and who was the most famous actor or gladiator in their coliseums (Luke 14:18-24). They were so busy with their lives, that they were oblivious to the fact that the One who created the stars was walking amongst them, offering them salvation (Colossians 1:16).

When the Creator stood before Herod, the only interest this secular leader had was to be entertained by a miracle. The reports of Jesus' ministry had been told to Herod (Luke 9:7-11), and when Jesus failed to entertain him, he passed Him over to be mocked and returned to Pilate (Luke 23:11-12).

In our culture, we too make the mistake of Herod. We are often busy with the temporal nonsense of who's who, what's in, or with the power struggles of politics. Occasionally, we may want to be entertained by God and blessed, but like the Roman leader Felix, we often treat Christ and His message as 'a distraction' from our plans. As Paul, 'Reasoned about righteousness, self-control and the judgment to come, Felix was afraid and answered, "Go away for now; when I have a convenient time I will call for you" ' (Acts 24:25).

We too dismiss the judgment to come, forgetting we have a temporal lease of life (Psalm 144:3-4). Today, we may bury an old friend, but in the blink of God's eye, we too will be buried (Psalm 90:4). To prepare for eternity we must wake up, dethrone our wills, feelings and thoughts and enthrone God. 'It is high time to awake out of sleep' (Romans 13:11).

Day 86

The Lord's Death

'Pilate brought Jesus out and sat down in the judgment seat in a place that is called The Pavement, but in Hebrew, Gabbatha. Now it was the Preparation Day of the Passover, and about the sixth hour. And he said to the Jews, "Behold your King!" But they cried out, "Away with Him, away with Him! Crucify Him!" Pilate said to them, "Shall I crucify your King?" The chief priests answered, "We have no king but Caesar!" Then he delivered Him to them to be crucified. Then they took Jesus and led Him away. And He, bearing His cross, went out to a place called the Place of a Skull, which is called in Hebrew, Golgotha, where they crucified Him, and two others with Him, one on either side, and Jesus in the centre' (John 19:13-19).

Pilate, under pressure from the religious leaders and the mob, condemned Christ; even before Jesus' trials, the high priest Caiaphas had decided His fate. 'He said, "It is expedient for us that one man should die for the people and not that the whole nation should perish." Now this he did not say on his own authority; but being high priest that year he prophesied that Jesus would die for the nation and not for that nation only, but also that He would gather together in one the children of God who were scattered abroad' (John 11:49-52). Thus, Pilate condemned Jesus. 'And when they crucified Him, they divided His garments, casting lots for them to determine what every man should take. Now it was the third hour and they crucified Him. And the inscription of His accusation was written above: THE KING OF THE JEWS...And at the ninth hour Jesus cried out with a loud voice, saying, "Eloi, Eloi, lama sabachthani?" which is translated, "My God, My God, why have You forsaken Me?" ...And Jesus cried out with a loud voice, and breathed His last. Then the veil of the temple was torn in two from top to bottom. So when the centurion, who stood opposite Him, saw that He cried out like this and breathed His last, he said, "Truly this Man was the Son of God!" (Mark 15:24-26, 34, 37-39). Then, to fulfil prophecy, Jesus' body was taken down and buried in a rich man's tomb (Mark 15:42-47).

Day 87

The Servant King

"For the Son of Man did not come to be served, but to serve and to give His life a ransom for many" (Mark 10:45).

Jesus came to earth to be the Servant King. The Jewish leaders of His day knew many of the prophecies of the coming Messiah, but they failed to comprehend the fullness of God's plan. The Jews were looking for a king who would rid the nation of Roman rule and restore the Kingdom of David (Acts 1:6). They embraced the prophecies of a great Kingdom, whilst neglecting Isaiah's Immanuel prophecy of, "God with us" (Isaiah 7:14, Matthew 1:23). They enjoyed the concept of a conquering king (Psalm 2:8-9, Revelation 19:11-16), but were not prepared for the Servant King, who came first to suffer, as the prophets foretold.

Isaiah said, "He was led as a lamb to the slaughter and as a sheep before its shearers is silent, so He opened not His mouth. He was taken from prison and from judgment, and who will declare His generation? For He was cut off from the land of the living. For the transgressions of My people He was stricken and they made His grave with the wicked – but with the rich at His death, because He had done no violence, nor was any deceit in His mouth" (Isaiah 53:7-9).

Jesus foretold His suffering, death and resurrection many times; He knew He was, 'The Lamb slain from the foundation of the world' (Revelation 13:8). This was God's plan from the beginning. At least eight times in the Gospels we are told of the importance of the Scriptures being fulfilled (Matthew 26:54-56, Mark 14:49, John 13:18, 17:12, 19:24, 28, 36), and the apostles declared, "Those things which God foretold by the mouth of all His prophets, that the Christ would suffer, He has thus fulfilled" (Acts 3:18).

Why did Christ come? "I have come down from heaven, not to do My own will, but the will of Him who sent Me. This is the will of the Father who sent Me, that of all He has given Me I should lose nothing, but should raise it up at the last day. And this is the will of Him who sent Me, that everyone who sees the Son and believes in Him may have everlasting life; and I will raise him up at the last day" (John 6:38-40).

Day 88

As It Is Written

"You say rightly that I am a King. For this cause I was born and for this cause I have come into the world, that I should bear witness to the truth. Everyone who is of the truth hears My voice" (John 18:37).

I often perceive prophecy as a two-sided coin. If we are not careful, we can look exclusively at one-side of the coin and miss the other, leading to a distorted unequal view of what God has said (1 Corinthians 13:9). The Jews were looking for a king and they were right to look for one; but first this King was to manifest Himself as the Suffering Servant, the bearer of all Truth, to fulfil prophecy. It was after His death and resurrection that John heard the title of, 'The King of Kings and Lord of Lords' (Revelation 19:16). Christ came from heaven to establish an eternal Kingdom, not another temporary Jewish Kingdom. Jesus said, "My Kingdom is not of this world…My Kingdom is not from here" (John 18:36).

Christ came to fulfil all the prophecies concerning Him and over forty times in the New Testament it states: 'As it is written.' Jesus knew His mission was to fulfil prophecy: "The Son of Man indeed goes just as it is written of Him" (Matthew 26:24). Jesus was born of a virgin (Isaiah 7:14, Luke 1:26-31), ministered in Galilee (Isaiah 9:1-2, Matthew 4:13-16), and is heir to David's throne (Isaiah 9:7, Luke 1:32-33). His coming was foretold (Isaiah 40:3-5, John 1:19-28), He would suffer (Isaiah 50:6, Matthew 26:67), and be exalted (Isaiah 52:13, Philippians 2:9). During His Passion He was to be beaten and mocked (Isaiah 52:14, Mark 15:15-19), as He made atonement for sins (Isaiah 53:5, 1 Peter 1:2). He was to be rejected by His people (Isaiah 53:1-4, John 12:37-38), as He sacrificed His life (Isaiah 53:4-5, Romans 4:25). The Messiah would silently embrace His death (Isaiah 53:7, Mark 15:4), and would be buried with the rich (Isaiah 53:9, John 19:38-42). Afterwards, the Messiah would rise from the dead as a victor and all in the future will be subject to Him (Isaiah 53:12, Philippians 2:10).

Jesus testified, "But all this was done that the Scriptures of the prophets might be fulfilled" (Matthew 26:56).

Day 89

The First Witnesses of the Resurrection

'Now after the Sabbath, as the first day of the week began to dawn, Mary Magdalene and the other Mary came to see the tomb. And behold, there was a great earthquake; for an angel of the Lord descended from heaven, and came and rolled back the stone from the door and sat on it. His countenance was like lightning and his clothing as white as snow. And the guards shook for fear of him, and became like dead men. But the angel answered and said to the women, "Do not be afraid, for I know that you seek Jesus who was crucified. He is not here; for He is risen, as He said. Come, see the place where the Lord lay. And go quickly and tell His disciples that He is risen from the dead, and indeed He is going before you into Galilee; there you will see Him. Behold, I have told you." So they went out quickly from the tomb with fear and great joy, and ran to bring His disciples word. And as they went to tell His disciples, behold, Jesus met them, saying, "Rejoice!" So they came and held Him by the feet and worshiped Him. Then Jesus said to them, "Do not be afraid. Go and tell My brethren to go to Galilee and there they will see Me" ' (Matthew 28:1-10).

After the terror of the cross, the prophecies of the Messiah being raised from the dead came to pass (Luke 24:25-27). The first to know this glorious news was not the male disciples who were hiding in fear, but the faithful women and this is a wonderful picture of God's grace toward women.

Women were the first to see and know of the resurrected Christ, and they were commissioned by the Lord to tell the men. 'Then they returned from the tomb and told all these things to the eleven and to all the rest. It was Mary Magdalene, Joanna, Mary the mother of James and the other women with them, who told these things to the apostles' (Luke 24:9-11).

Later on, in the Upper Room prayer meetings after Christ's ascension, Mary the mother of Jesus and other women were present as they sought God in preparation for the Spirit's outpouring and the Spirit came upon all (Acts 1:12, 2:1-4).

Day 90

Disciples of Jesus Observe All

'Jesus came and spoke to them, saying, "All authority has been given to Me in heaven and on earth. Go therefore and make disciples of all the nations, baptizing them in the name of the Father and of the Son and of the Holy Spirit, teaching them to observe all things that I have commanded you; and lo, I am with you always, even to the end of the age" ' (Matthew 28:18-20).

When Jesus Christ completed His earthly ministry, He commanded His followers to make disciples of all nations. Jesus also explained what discipleship means through His teaching and in His parting words. Jesus' disciples must be taught, "To observe all things that I have commanded you."

There is a great distinction between Sunday Christianity and Jesus' description of discipleship. To be a disciple of Jesus means placing all at His feet, to be available for His disposal whenever He chooses. It means getting off the inner throne of our hearts and allowing Christ to sit there. It means removing ourselves from the axis of self, which we have spun around all of our lives, and welcoming the Holy Spirit to be the One who guides us into God's will.

Jesus said, "Whoever does not bear his cross and come after Me cannot be My disciple. For which of you, intending to build a tower, does not sit down first and count the cost, whether he has enough to finish it – lest, after he has laid the foundation, and is not able to finish, all who see it begin to mock him, saying, 'This man began to build and was not able to finish' " (Luke 14:27-31).

The kind of Christianity which requires one hour of our time on Sunday and a few daily rituals is no Christianity. It is anathema to God (Amos 5:21-24). Faith in Christ must consume us and define every area of our lives. This is what discipleship means – giving Him everything and following Him all the way to the cross, and into His resurrection.

Christ provides us with many great promises and one is the hope of entering into His eternal realm of heaven to share His glory, but to do so, we must trade our rags for His eternal riches (Ephesians 4:22-24). Are you Jesus' disciple?

Day 91

Christ's Ascension Into Heaven

'Now as they said these things, Jesus Himself stood in the midst of them and said to them, "Peace to you." But they were terrified and frightened, and supposed they had seen a spirit. And He said to them, "Why are you troubled? And why do doubts arise in your hearts? Behold My hands and My feet, that it is I Myself. Handle Me and see, for a spirit does not have flesh and bones as you see I have." When He had said this, He showed them His hands and His feet. But while they still did not believe for joy and marvelled...Then He said to them, "These are the words which I spoke to you while I was still with you, that all things must be fulfilled which were written in the Law of Moses and the Prophets and the Psalms concerning Me." And He opened their understanding, that they might comprehend the Scriptures.'

'Then He said to them, "Thus it is written, and thus it was necessary for the Christ to suffer and to rise from the dead the third day, and that repentance and remission of sins should be preached in His name to all nations, beginning at Jerusalem. And you are witnesses of these things...Behold, I send the promise of My Father upon you; but tarry in the city of Jerusalem until you are endued with power from on high." And He led them out as far as Bethany and He lifted up His hands and blessed them. Now it came to pass, while He blessed them, that He was parted from them and carried up into heaven. And they worshiped Him and returned to Jerusalem with great joy, and were continually in the temple praising and blessing God. Amen' (Luke 24:36-53).

After His resurrection, Jesus appeared to His disciples and opened their minds to understand all the biblical prophecies concerning His suffering, resurrection and glorification. He told them to wait for the promise of the Spirit and was taken up into heaven. There was only one thing the disciples could do – they worshiped Him. Jesus continues to live and abide in heaven as God, where He intercedes for His Church (Romans 8:34, Hebrews 7:25). Jesus Christ now looks to His Father to tell Him when to return to earth (Acts 1:11), and every knee will bow before Him (Philippians 2:10).

Day 92

What Does it Mean?

"Father, I desire that they also whom You gave Me may be with Me where I am, that they may behold My glory which You have given Me; for You loved Me before the foundation of the world. O righteous Father! The world has not known You, but I have known You; and these have known that You sent Me. And I have declared to them Your name and will declare it, that the love with which You loved Me may be in them, and I in them" (John 17:24-26).

It is possible to divide the Bible into three sections of God's plan for redemption. The Old Testament looks forward to Christ, the Gospels tell the story of Christ's life, and the rest of the New Testament explains what Jesus' death and resurrection means, and how its application will change all.

When Jesus prayed for His disciples before He ascended into heaven, He asked for them to join Him, "That they may behold My glory which You have given Me." Meanwhile on earth, the Holy Spirit continues the ministry of Jesus (John 16:13). Through the power of the Holy Spirit Jesus continued to reveal Himself to people. The Lord spoke to Paul saying, "I am Jesus, whom you are persecuting" (Acts 9:5), and Paul became His disciple. Then through a series of revelations (Romans 16:25, Galatians 2:2), Paul was taught by the Holy Spirit the significance of Jesus' Passion and His coming back to life, and wrote explaining what it all means.

Christ 'was sacrificed for us' (1 Corinthians 5:7). He was, 'Declared to be the Son of God with power according to the Spirit of Holiness, by the resurrection from the dead' (Romans 1:4). Now, if we believe in our hearts that God raised Jesus from the dead, we will be saved (Romans 10:9). Therefore, 'We who once were far off have been brought near by the blood of Christ' (Ephesians 2:13). Death has been defeated and we will be raised, 'In the likeness of His resurrection' (Romans 6:5). We are, 'Heirs of God and joint heirs with Christ' (Romans 8:17). We are new creations who have been reconciled to God; we are His witnesses and ambassadors on earth (2 Corinthians 5:17-19). 'If God is for us, who can be against us?' (Romans 8:31).

Day 93

The Beginning of the Sorrows

"Take heed that no one deceives you. For many will come in My name, saying, 'I am He,' and will deceive many. But when you hear of wars and rumours of wars, do not be troubled; for such things must happen, but the end is not yet. For nation will rise against nation and kingdom against kingdom. And there will be earthquakes in various places, and there will be famines and troubles. These are the beginnings of sorrows. But watch out for yourselves, for they will deliver you up to councils and you will be beaten in the synagogues. You will be brought before rulers and kings for My sake, for a testimony to them. And the gospel must first be preached to all the nations. But when they arrest you and deliver you up, do not worry beforehand, or premeditate what you will speak. But whatever is given you in that hour, speak that; for it is not you who speak, but the Holy Spirit. Now brother will betray brother to death and a father his child; and children will rise up against parents and cause them to be put to death. And you will be hated by all for My name's sake. But he who endures to the end shall be saved" (Mark 13:5-13).

Before Jesus ascended into heaven, He gave us a detailed description of the end times (Matthew 24-25, Mark 13, Luke 21). Christ will return to earth to complete the redemption of those who trusted in Him, and He will also rule and reign for a millennium, when we will discover what life could have been like, if mankind had not fallen (Revelation 20:4-5).

Prior to this, Christ describes a period of great deception on earth with many religious systems and multiple claims of spiritual leaders, and messiahs. There will be an increase in wars, earthquakes, famines and troubles. All this is just the beginning. As the end comes closer, persecution against Christ's true followers by the authorities will increase. Public opinion will be hostile to the faith and believers will be hated by many, with families divided over their faith in Christ and betrayals taking place. Look to the news around the world and see these things! Meanwhile, the gospel must first be preached to all nations; and we must endure to the end!

Day 94

The Rapture

"For as the lightning comes from the east and flashes to the west, so also will the coming of the Son of Man be. For wherever the carcass is, there the eagles will be gathered together" (Matthew 24:27-28).

In a short passage in Matthew 24:27-31, Jesus describes that He will first come for His Church in a 'lightning' strike (Matthew 24:27-28), and will later come for all to see Him, with His angels to rule and reign (Matthew 24:30-31).

When Christ first comes for His Church in a lightning strike, believers will be on earth one second and gone before the next. Non-believers will not see Jesus Christ and they will not understand what has happened. The antichrist may well use this confusion to his advantage (2 Thessalonians 2:3). Jesus' reference concerning, "The eagles will be gathered together," may imply the forthcoming battles between people for the possessions of the raptured believers.

Jesus said, "I will come again and receive you to Myself, that where I am, there you may be also" (John 14:3). 'For the Lord Himself will descend from heaven with a shout, with the voice of an archangel and with the trumpet of God. And the dead in Christ will rise first. Then we who are alive and remain shall be caught up together with them in the clouds to meet the Lord in the air' (1 Thessalonians 4:16-17).

This is called the Resurrection of the Just by Jesus Christ (Luke 14:14), or by Paul, the Day of Redemption (Ephesians 4:30), and the Day of Christ (Philippians 2:16). Only at this point will believers in Jesus achieve the total redemption of their persons; with every spirit, soul and body completely redeemed (1 Corinthians 15:51-57, 1 John 3:2).

After our resurrection, the Judgment of Believers will begin, called the Judgment Seat of Christ (Romans 14:10-12, 2 Corinthians 5:10, 2 Timothy 4:1). This judgment determines rewards for faithfulness, not access to salvation (2 Timothy 4:8). Believers will be judged, 'According to each one's work' (1 Peter 1:17), and God will test the purity of our works (1 Corinthians 3:10-15, 1 Peter 1:7-9). In heaven believers will wait to return with Jesus (1 Thessalonians 3:13, Jude 14).

Day 95

The Antichrist

"So when you see the 'abomination of desolation,' spoken of by Daniel the prophet, standing where it ought not" (let the reader understand), "then let those who are in Judea flee to the mountains. Let him who is on the housetop not go down into the house, nor enter to take anything out of his house. And let him who is in the field not go back to get his clothes. But woe to those who are pregnant and to those who are nursing babies in those days! And pray that your flight may not be in winter. For in those days there will be tribulation, such as has not been since the beginning of the creation which God created until this time, nor ever shall be. And unless the Lord had shortened those days, no flesh would be saved; but for the elect's sake, whom He chose, He shortened the days. Then if anyone says to you, 'Look, here is the Christ!' or, 'Look, He is there!' do not believe it. For false christs and false prophets will rise and show signs and wonders to deceive, if possible, even the elect. But take heed; see, I have told you all things beforehand" (Mark 13:14-21).

Some theologians think the rapture of believers will happen before the great period of the tribulation, others during or after. Nevertheless, Jesus notes that an abomination will be present on earth where it ought not. He was referencing Daniel's prophecy concerning the defilement of the Jewish temple (Daniel 9:27, 11:31, 12:11), when sacrifices will be stopped. This seems to indicate that a third Jewish temple will be built in the future and the antichrist – the physical embodiment of all rebellion against God – will sit inside the temple to be praised like a God. This is the abomination.

Paul wrote of this to the Thessalonians. 'For that Day will not come unless the falling away comes first and the man of sin is revealed, the son of perdition (the antichrist), who opposes and exalts himself above all that is called God or that is worshiped, so that he sits as God in the temple of God, showing himself that he is God' (2 Thessalonians 2:3-4). This evil man will be empowered by Satan and will rule a worldwide antichrist government (Revelation 13:2-7).

Day 96

The Second Coming

"But in those days, after that tribulation, the sun will be darkened and the moon will not give its light; the stars of heaven will fall, and the powers in the heavens will be shaken. Then they will see the Son of Man coming in the clouds with great power and glory. And then He will send His angels and gather together His elect from the four winds, from the farthest part of earth to the farthest part of heaven" (Mark 13:24-27).

The antichrist will most probably be a popular political leader of a world union of governments, and during his rule, a period of intense tribulation will be experienced on earth, to the extent that the sun and moon will be darkened, and stars will fall from the sky. Jesus in heaven will break open the seven end time seals, which will lead to many judgments (Revelation 6:1-7:8). There will be great judgments – seven great trumpets and seven bowls of wrath (Revelation 8:7-11:19, 16:2-20), and Israel will also be restored (Acts 1:6-8).

The purpose of this intense judgment is to wake people out of their spiritual slumber, to encourage them to repent (Romans 13:11), and to cleanse the world of its wickedness. During this era a great multitude of people will be saved (Revelation 7:9-17), due to the witness of 144,000 Jewish evangelists (Revelation 7:4-8). Just as the proclamation of the gospel began with Jews, it will end with Jews too. 'Now if their fall is riches for the world and their failure riches for the Gentiles, how much more their fullness!' (Romans 11:12).

Christ will then return to be seen by all in His glory, with His armies (Revelation 19:11-15). The antichrist and his armies will be gathered to Megiddo and defeated (Revelation 19:17-21); Satan will be bound (Revelation 20:1-3), and Christ will rule on earth for one thousand years (Revelation 20:4-6). At the start of His reign, Christ will judge all the nations.

Jesus said, "When the Son of Man comes in His glory, and all the holy angels with Him, then He will sit on the throne of His glory. All the nations will be gathered before Him and He will separate them one from another, as a shepherd divides his sheep from the goats..." (Matthew 25:31-33).

Day 97

The Day and the Hour is Not Known

"But of that day and hour no one knows, not even the angels in heaven, nor the Son, but only the Father. Take heed, watch and pray; for you do not know when the time is. It is like a man going to a far country, who left his house and gave authority to his servants, and to each his work and commanded the doorkeeper to watch. Watch therefore, for you do not know when the master of the house is coming – in the evening, at midnight, at the crowing of the rooster, or in the morning, lest, coming suddenly, he find you sleeping. And what I say to you, I say to all: Watch!" (Mark 13:32-37).

Christians live in the state of being in flux between two very real and alternative realities (Hebrews 9:27). The first reality is the temporal civilisations and bodies we inhabit on earth; the second is the eternal invisible reality of Christ's heaven, to which all peoples will be held accountable (1 Peter 4:5).

If we allow ourselves to be unspiritual and never take heed to Jesus' teaching, we may decide, 'What is real,' simply by what our five senses tell us. If we do this, our lives could be consumed with all the temporal nonsense of, 'What's hot and what's not,' and the problems of politics, governments, entertainment, or the aspirations of the rich and famous, etc. If this is the only reality we perceive, it will be hard for us to see beyond this earth to the eternal invisible reality – but we must. The temporal reality will end; the eternal will go on and consume all. Joseph lived in ancient Egypt and its ruins survive today. Daniel lived in Babylon and Jesus lived on earth during the period of Roman power. The ruins of these civilisations remain, whilst the people who once lived in them are in heaven or hell, awaiting Judgment Day, and the return of Jesus Christ to earth – God's D-Day.

No-one on earth knows when Christ will return and all the guessing to find exact dates will prove to be foolish, as many already have been. The Lord does not command us to guess the date, but to, "Watch." He will return when we do not expect Him (2 Peter 3:4). Just at the time when many are spiritually asleep, and are consumed with the temporal, and have almost forgotten about His return – then suddenly!

Day 98

The Everlasting Words of Christ

"Do not think that I came to destroy the Law or the Prophets. I did not come to destroy but to fulfil. For assuredly, I say to you, till heaven and earth pass away, one jot or one tittle will by no means pass from the Law till all is fulfilled. Whoever therefore breaks one of the least of these commandments and teaches men so, shall be called least in the Kingdom of Heaven; but whoever does and teaches them, he shall be called great in the Kingdom of Heaven" (Matthew 5:17-20).

We live in a world which will have a definitive end; but the words of Christ will endure. Jesus said, "Heaven and earth will pass away, but My words will by no means pass away" (Luke 21:33). At some future point, God will start again and put right what mankind made wrong on planet earth one.

'Now I saw a new heaven and a new earth, for the first heaven and the first earth had passed away' (Revelation 21:1). John saw the new worlds God is going to create, and Peter foresaw the end of this reality of heaven and earth. 'Looking for and hastening the coming of the day of God, because of which the heavens will be dissolved being on fire and the elements will melt with fervent heat. Nevertheless we, according to His promise, look for new heavens and a new earth in which righteousness dwells' (2 Peter 3:12-13).

The new creation will forever be perfect and unspoiled, with righteousness at its core. Meanwhile, Christ's Kingdom already exists on earth in part, as He finds people who choose to serve Him freely (Luke 17:21, 1 John 4:19).

In Christ's eternal Kingdom there will be people who, "Shall be called least in the Kingdom of Heaven" and others who, "Shall be called great." The least will be those who, "Breaks one of the least of these commandments and teaches men so." Thus, our status in the next life will be determined by how we respond to and obey the commandments of Christ now (Matthew 16:27). Remember, the Law and the Prophets all point towards Christ. Thus, when we obey all of Christ's commands and encourage others to follow Him, we will be honoured in His Kingdom (Daniel 12:3, Revelation 22:12).

Day 99

Go Therefore

"Go therefore and make disciples of all the nations, baptizing them in the name of the Father and of the Son and of the Holy Spirit, teaching them to observe all things that I have commanded you; and lo, I am with you always, even to the end of the age" (Matthew 28:19-20).

Planet earth one presently abides in days of grace, as God holds back His eternal plans, giving mankind time to repent, so the fullness of His 'big catch' of souls can be completed (Mark 1:17, Acts 2:17-21). Meanwhile, everyday people from this generation walk across the invisible line into the eternal reality of God, made visible through death (Psalm 104:29, Hebrews 9:27). Heaven or hell is awaiting them and it awaits us too. But why does God delay His end time plans? God says, "I have no pleasure in the death of the wicked, but that the wicked turn from his way and live. Turn, turn from your evil ways! For why should you die?" (Ezekiel 33:11).

In the days of the apostles, some scoffers began to ask why Jesus had yet to return and Peter wrote to explain that heaven and earth, 'Are reserved for fire until the Day of Judgment and perdition of ungodly men' (2 Peter 3:7). Nevertheless, in God's eternal perspective a thousand years is as only one day (2 Peter 3:8). Even if Christ's return was in two thousand years from Peter's day, it would only be two days to God! Peter also explained the reason for God's patience. 'The Lord is not slack concerning His promise, as some count slackness, but is longsuffering toward us, not willing that any should perish, but that all should come to repentance' (2 Peter 3:9). God is holding back His end time plans to give everyone in the world a chance to hear Christ's gospel and repent (Mark 16:15-18).

Jesus said, "This gospel of the Kingdom will be preached in all the world as a witness to all the nations and then the end will come" (Matthew 24:14). When the Church obeys its Master and seeks to reach the world with His gospel, it is, 'Hastening the coming of the day of God' (2 Peter 3:12). We thought we were waiting for Jesus' return, when in fact He is waiting for us, His Church, to obey His last command.

Day 100

Those who Sow and Reap

"My food is to do the will of Him who sent Me and to finish His work. Do you not say, 'There are still four months and then comes the harvest?' Behold, I say to you, lift up your eyes and look at the fields, for they are already white for harvest! And he who reaps receives wages and gathers fruit for eternal life, that both he who sows and he who reaps may rejoice together. For in this the saying is true: 'One sows and another reaps.' I sent you to reap that for which you have not labored; others have labored and you have entered into their labors" (John 4:34-38).

In His Great Commission, Christ lays a duty of obedience upon all believers to do their part in sending the gospel to every person in the world. Jesus said, "Go into all the world and preach the gospel to every creature. He who believes and is baptized will be saved; but he who does not believe will be condemned" (Mark 16:15-17).

The Lord also warns us not to make excuses for not being involved (Luke 21:34, John 4:35). Christ explains there is a harvest now taking place and believers should be separated into two groups: those who sow and those who reap. In the West, with our selfish consumer culture we tend to project this worldview onto our faith, leaving us with inward looking churches. We find it hard to be Kingdom minded and want to know, "What will I, my church and my ministry get from....?" But Christ's vision, His eternal Kingdom and His Church are global. Jesus said, "Other sheep I have which are not of this fold; them also I must bring and they will hear My voice; and there will be one flock and One Shepherd" (John 10:16).

Consequently, if we are to obey the Lord's last command, we must take personal responsibility and ask, "What am I doing to obey the Great Commission?" Today, there are millions of believers in developing countries who cannot afford a Bible and countless poor local evangelists who are called to reach their people with the gospel. Can you help? What has God called you to do? Are you obeying? There is a harvest! We must, "Finish His work" (John 4:34).

This book is also available as an ebook.

Books by the Author

- *Holy Spirit Power: Knowing the Voice, Guidance and Person of the Holy Spirit*
- *Heaven: A Journey to Paradise and the Heavenly City*
- *The End Times: A Journey Through the Last Days. The Book of Revelation*
- *The Exodus Evidence In Pictures – The Bible's Exodus:* 100+ colour photos
- *The Ark of the Covenant – Investigating the Ten Leading Claims:* 80+ colour photos
- *Jesus Today, Daily Devotional: 100 Days with Jesus Christ*
- *How Christianity Made the Modern World*
- *Britain, A Christian Country*
- *Celtic Christianity and the First Christian Kings in Britain*
- The Baptism of Fire, Personal Revival and the Anointing for Supernatural Living
- Glimpses of Glory, Revelations in the Realms of God
- Lost Treasures of the Bible
- *Samuel Rees Howells: A Life of Intercession* by Richard Maton, with Paul and Mathew Backholer

Revival Fires and Awakenings – Thirty-Six Visitations of the Holy Spirit by Mathew Backholer.

Reformation to Revival, 500 Years of God's Glory: Sixty Revivals, Awakenings and Heaven-Sent Visitations of the Holy Spirit by Mathew Backholer

How to Plan, Prepare and Successfully Complete Your Short-Term Mission by Mathew Backholer.

Revival Fire – 150 Years of Revivals by Mathew Backholer documents twelve revivals from ten countries.

Discipleship for Everyday Living by Mathew Backholer. A dynamic biblical book for Christian growth.

Global Revival, Worldwide Outpourings, Forty-Three Visitations of the Holy Spirit by Mathew Backholer.

Understanding Revival and Addressing the Issues it Provokes by Mathew Backholer.

Extreme Faith – On Fire Christianity by Mathew Backholer. Powerful foundations for faith in Christ!

Revival Answers: True and False Revivals by Mathew Backholer. What is genuine and false revival?

Short-Term Missions, A Christian Guide to STMs, For Leaders, Pastors, Students... by Mathew Backholer.

Budget Travel, A Guide to Travelling on a Shoestring Explore the World by Mathew Backholer

Prophecy Now, Prophetic Words and Divine Revelations, For You, the Church and the Nations by Michael Backholer.

Samuel Rees Howells: A Life of Intercession by Richard Maton. Learn how intercession and prayer changed history.

Samuel, Son and Successor of Rees Howells by Richard Maton. Discover the full biography of Samuel Rees Howells.

The Holy Spirit in a Man by R.B. Watchman. An autobiography.

Tares and Weeds in your Church: Trouble & Deception in God's House by R.B. Watchman.

How Christianity Made the Modern World by Paul Backholer.

Holy Spirit Power: Knowing the Voice, Guidance and Person of the Holy Spirit by Paul Backholer.

Heaven: A Journey to Paradise and the Heavenly City by Paul Backholer.

The Exodus Evidence In Pictures – The Bible's Exodus by Paul Backholer. 100+ colour photos.

The Ark of the Covenant – Investigating the Ten Leading Claims by Paul Backholer. 80+ colour photos.

Britain, A Christian Country by Paul Backholer.

Celtic Christianity and the First Christian Kings in Britain by Paul Backholer.

The Baptism of Fire, Personal Revival and the Anointing for Supernatural Living by Paul Backholer.

Glimpses of Glory, Revelations in the Realms of God by Paul Backholer

Lost Treasures of the Bible by Paul Backholer.

The End Times: A Journey Through the Last Days. The Book of Revelation…by Paul Backholer.

Debt Time Bomb! Debt Mountains: The Financial Crisis and its Toxic Legacy by Paul Backholer. Ebook.

www.ByFaithBooks.co.uk

ByFaith Media DVDs

Great Christian Revivals on 1 DVD is an uplifting account of some of the greatest revivals in Church history. Filmed on location across Britain and drawing upon archive information, the stories of the Welsh Revival (1904-1905), the Hebridean Revival (1949-1952) and the Evangelical Revival (1739-1791), are told in this 72 minute documentary.

ByFaith – Quest for the Ark of the Covenant on 1 DVD. Experience an adventure and investigate the mystery of the lost Ark of the Covenant! Explore Ethiopia's rock churches; find the Egyptian Pharaoh who entered Solomon's Temple and search for the Queen of Sheba's Palace. Four episodes. 100+ minutes.

ByFaith – World Mission on 1 DVD. Pack your backpack and join two adventurers as they travel through 14 nations on their global short-term mission (STM). Get inspired for your STM, as you watch this 85 minute adventure; filmed over three years.

Israel in Egypt – The Exodus Mystery on 1 DVD. A four year quest searching for the evidence for Joseph, Moses and the Hebrew Slaves in Egypt. Explore the Exodus route, hunt for the Red Sea and climb Mount Sinai. This is the best of the eight episode TV series *ByFaith – In Search of the Exodus.* 110+ minutes.

ByFaith – In Search of the Exodus on 2 DVDs. The quest to find the evidence for ancient Israel in Egypt, the Red Sea and Mount Sinai, in eight TV episodes. 200+ minutes.

Visit **www.ByFaith.org** to watch the trailers for these DVDs and for more information.

www.ByFaithDVDs.co.uk

Notes